Xmas /

HEROES & V
OF KEN

HEROES & VILLAINS OF KENT

Adrian Gray

COUNTRYSIDE BOOKS
NEWBURY, BERKSHIRE

First Published 1989
© Adrian Gray 1989

COUNTRYSIDE BOOKS
3 Catherine Road
Newbury, Berkshire

ISBN 1 85306 060 7

Produced through MRM Associates, Reading
Typeset by Acorn Bookwork, Salisbury
Printed in England by J W Arrowsmith Ltd., Bristol

Bibliography

P Allderidge: 'The Late Richard Dadd': 1974
Archaeologica Cantiana: 1965
M Baldwin: 'The River and The Downs': 1984
F Barlow: 'Thomas Becket': 1986
P Beresford-Ellis: 'Caesar's Invasion of Britain': 1978
Butler's Lives of the Fathers, Martyrs & Saints
E M Cobham: 'The Siege of Cooling': 1896
Dictionary of National Biography
M Duffy: 'The Passionate Shepherdess': 1977
J Forster: 'Life of Dickens'
R Furneaux: 'The Seven Years War': 1973
I Guest: 'Napoleon III in England': 1952
J Guy: 'Kent Castles': 1980
E W Ives: 'Anne Boleyn': 1986
Kent Life
A J Mason: 'The Mission of St Augustine to England': 1897
A Neame: 'The Holy Maid of Kent': 1971
J G Nichols: 'Chronicle of Queen Jane': 1850
W N Nichols: 'Cooling & Its Castle': 1980
U Pope-Hennessy: 'Charles Dickens': 1945
P C Rogers: 'The First Englishman in Japan': 1956
J Simson: 'Eminent Men of Kent': 1893
Victoria County History
R Webber: 'The Peasants' Revolt': 1980
A Winnifrith: 'Fair Maids of Kent': 1921

Contents

THOMAS BECKET
MARTYR OF CANTERBURY

BECKET is a name deeply engraved into the history of Kent and forever associated with the city of Canterbury. Without Becket there would have been no *Canterbury Tales* and probably the city itself would be very different – for its wealth in the Middle Ages was due, in no small degree, to the thriving pilgrimage trade that Becket's death encouraged. Those were the days when monks would steal holy relics from each other in order to attract pilgrims, but Canterbury had the most famous relics of all. However, the image of Becket as a pious and saintly man murdered on the orders of a wicked king does not quite fit the reality of his story.

Born in about 1120, Thomas Becket was the son of a prosperous London merchant. He was thus in a position to be educated and to get a suitable post in a rich man's household, allowing him plenty of opportunity for youthful exploits. On one occasion he went hawking in Sussex, fell into a millstream and nearly drowned. He rounded off his education with a short spell in Paris, returning home in 1141.

From 1143 to 1145 he served a London banker named Osbert Eightpence, before joining the staff of Theobald, the Archbishop of Canterbury. For an ambitious young man the Church offered a good career. It had money, there were ample opportunities to exploit the patronage system if you knew the right people, and it conferred access to the most powerful people in the land. Becket soon began to find that his personal charm could at least open the door of patronage, and he secured the benefice of Otford – this brought him revenue without his having to do any duties, though he was not even ordained a priest. In 1154 he became Archdeacon of Canterbury, earning a princely salary of £100 a year.

In 1154 King Henry II was crowned and Becket became his Chancellor. It was the start of a period of high-living, during which Becket kept wolves and monkeys as pets and was rich enough to make Henry a present of three ships. Perhaps he suffered from his conscience however, since he made periodic visits to St Martin's in Canterbury for 'discipline' – scourging.

In 1159 Becket revealed new talents by leading a military campaign in Aquitaine during which the town of Cahors was recaptured, but the real turning point in his career came with the death of Theobald in 1161. Henry chose Becket to be the next Archbishop, though there was a slight handicap – Becket was still a layman! A hasty ordination was arranged for 2nd June 1162 and the following day Becket was consecrated a bishop at Canterbury – a truly meteoric rise through the clerical ranks!

Once Archbishop, Becket's personality seemed to change, though he never really got rid of a bad temper and a penchant for abusive language. He appeared to set aside his worldly ways and became a fierce advocate of the Church's rights, which had been gradually eroded by the monarchy. Some of the other bishops, not surprisingly, suspected Becket of hypocrisy over this. He astonished the people of Canterbury by washing the feet of 13 poor men every night at 2am, then surprised Henry by demanding custody of the castles at Rochester, Hythe and Saltwood. The people of Tonbridge were told that they must pay to him the homage that they owed under the feudal system.

By 1163 Becket seemed to be heading for a confrontation with

Inside Canterbury cathedral where Archbishop Thomas Becket was murdered on 29th December 1170.

King Henry. He refused to pay taxes to the monarch and Henry responded by backing Roger de Clare's claim that he was the rightful controller of the Tonbridge dues. Henry then sacked the man that Becket had appointed as vicar of Saltwood.

Another Kent parish to cause conflict was Eynsford. Becket appointed a vicar to whom the lord of the manor objected, so Becket excommunicated the lord! Henry intervened and forced Becket to retract this dire punishment.

Henry could now see that he had miscalculated. Becket had thrown himself so far into his new role that all hope of compromise had vanished. Henry had a growing list of objections to Becket's practices – the Church courts were too lenient, the laity were unfairly punished for moral offences, and the traditional 'rules' of church–state relations had been breached. In January 1164 Becket also banned the King's brother from marrying the Countess of Surrey.

Perhaps Becket now lost his nerve, for on 23rd August 1164 he left Canterbury and travelled via Aldington to Romney, where he took a boat for France. However, the sailors discovered who he was and realised that it was treason for the Archbishop to leave the country without the King's permission, so they took him back to Kent. Becket was taken to Northampton for trial, with many bishops whispering that his past sins were catching up with him.

The bishops tried to persuade Becket to give the King the manors of Otford and Wingham, but Becket said he had already been deprived of the revenues of Higham and that was quite enough. Becket was fined, then fled to Lincoln, Boston and down the east coast to Eastry in Kent. He reached France on 2nd November 1164.

The Pope was bombarded by letters of complaint from both King Henry and Becket. Becket won most of the arguments but dared not return, so Henry confiscated his benefices. Becket's stewards, Pain of Otford and Philip of Tonge, were fined.

Becket was marooned at Vezelay in France, able to do little except threaten to excommunicate Henry. He stubbornly refused to return to Henry's old pattern of church–state relations. In 1169 the two opponents almost met at Montmartre, but they were unable to cope with facing each other.

An uneasy peace was made in 1170 and in early winter Becket returned to England. Not everyone wanted him back – the Archbishop of York and the Sheriff of Kent were both his opponents. Becket was angry with the other bishops for having crowned Henry II's son as Henry III while Becket was in France. Now the Archbishop was back in England while Henry II was still in France; there were rumours that Becket intended to use this chance to depose Henry III.

Becket first stayed at Sandwich and then journeyed to Canterbury, being given a great reception in each village along the way. But he had fewer friends among the aristocracy. The Earl of Cornwall complained that Becket wanted to excommunicate everyone – 'So far but a few of us, soon all of us, will be sent to Hell because of this.' On 19th December Becket was seen to point to his neck and say, 'This is where the varlets will get me.' His prediction was wrong by several inches.

He made several journeys to London and back, during one of which he stopped at Wrotham and met a poor curate from Chiddingstone. The curate said that St Lawrence had commanded that his relics be given to Becket, and confirmed the truth of his vision by revealing miraculous knowledge about a split in Becket's hair shirt. Becket rewarded the curate with a chapel at Penshurst.

As Christmas approached the de Broc family of Saltwood Castle stood guard over Canterbury, anxious to keep Becket in his nest where he could do little trouble. He preached in the cathedral on Christmas Day but some of the bishops went to France to petition Henry II about him. Henry was furious that Becket had suspended many of them and uttered his fateful words:

'What miserable drones and traitors have I nourished and promoted in my household, who let their lord be treated with such shameful contempt by a low-born clerk?'

The 'Dark Entry', a passage that leads on one side to the cloisters from where Becket and his assailants entered the cathedral.

Four knights, led by Reginald FitzUrse, decided to act. They left France and reached Saltwood by 28th December – but that they originally intended to murder Becket seems unlikely.

On their first meeting with Becket he chose to insult them by remaining seated when they entered the room. A heated discussion about the suspended bishops then followed. Not all of Becket's supporters were impressed by his tactics. One of them, John of Salisbury, told him that 'No-one here wants to die for the sake of dying except you.' Becket seems to have cast himself in the role of martyr and perhaps now was intent on fulfilling his part.

That night the knights returned and broke into the palace. They followed Becket into the cathedral where he called out, 'Here I am. No traitor to the King, but a priest of God.' He could have escaped into the crypt but stood his ground as a crowd gathered, trading insults with the knights in most unpriestly language. The knights tried to arrest him and a struggle broke out. FitzUrse struck him on the head with his sword, then finished the deed as Becket collapsed to the ground. It was 29th December 1170 and the Archbishop was dead. The sword that killed him clattered against the flagstones and broke in two.

Becket's body was taken to the altar but one of the de Brocs threatened to drag it through the streets. Richard of Dover decided to bury it immediately, and it was then that Becket's underwear of a hair shirt was discovered – alive with lice and worms.

The murderers escaped to Malling and then Knaresborough, but the cult of the martyr had already begun. On 4th January 1171 a blind woman recovered her sight due to a touch of Becket's bloodstained rags. Water tinctured with his blood was given to the sick to drink and worked so successfully that in March the de Brocs tried to steal the body.

Becket was canonised on 21st February 1173. In July 1174 Henry II arrived from London, dismounted at Harbledown and walked into Canterbury. At St Dunstan's he took off his boots and made a public confession. He wore a hair shirt and was 'beaten' by monks.

The death of Becket became the fortune of many Canterbury people. Until the Reformation, the city enjoyed a prosperous livelihood from pilgrims. English literature gained *The Canterbury Tales* and *Murder in the Cathedral*. But Becket himself was far from being a pure-minded martyr; he was a complex man whose sudden change in personality perplexed his patron Henry II and ultimately led to his death. Like many others, Henry was never to understand what had changed his old friend.

JULIUS CAESAR'S
GREAT INVASION

J ULIUS Caesar claimed to be descended from Venus but the
people who lived in Kent during his time had no reason to
associate him with love and romance, for he twice invaded
the area and dealt the British tribes a severe blow. Caesar's
origins were rather more earthly than he liked to claim, for he
was born in Rome in 102BC, the son of a government official.
Due to the style of his birth, the word 'caesarian' entered our
language.

By the age of 14 the young Caesar was a 'priest', but his
ambitions were also more earthly. He married Cornelia and
trained as a lawyer before joining the Army. By 74BC a successful military career had helped him win a place as a Senator and
his position was helped by his role in defeating Spartacus' slave
revolt in 71BC.

In 68BC he was placed in command of Spain, but he still had
time for a number of notorious affairs. There was a rumour that
Brutus was his son, and more officially he was able to marry
Pompeia and Calpurnia in quick succession.

In 60BC he was elected a Consul and the following year was
appointed Governor of Gaul, one of Rome's most important
provinces. It was also difficult, for the Gallic tribes were turbu-

lent and resented the Romans. Caesar's military genius soon proved equal to the task of pacifying the Gauls; the hallmarks of his style were very good relations with his troops and high speed movements to surprise the enemy.

His experience in Gaul made him familiar with the name of 'Britannia' – the 'tin island'. The Britons had often helped the rebel Gauls and so Caesar felt they deserved punishment, but he had also heard stories about the legendary wealth of these islands that lay at the edge of the known world. Caesar the politician could also see political advantages in being the first Roman to take on the Britons – supposed to be barbaric and dangerous.

In August 55BC Caesar prepared for the expedition. He gathered two legions at Wissant in northern France and set sail on 24th August. His galleys headed across the Channel towards the cliffs of the South Foreland.

Caesar intended to land in what is now Kent, then the home of the Cantii, a tribe which even Julius Caesar treated with respect. 'Of all the Britons,' he wrote, 'those that inhabit the lands of the Cantii are the most civilised.' They were certainly civilised enough to be well-organised and on 25th August were waiting on the clifftops as Caesar's fleet got its first sight of Britain. The Cantii had also arranged for some men from another tribe, the Atrebates, to reinforce them.

The cliffs made it impossible for the Romans to land at the South Foreland so their ships turned north. The Cantii leaders – Cingetorix, Carnilius, Taximagulus and Segonax – encouraged their men to shadow the Roman movements from dry land.

Caesar chose a spot near Walmer to come ashore, but the Cantii had gathered a hostile reception party. The Roman soldiers hesitated to fight their way ashore through the waves, only committing themselves when the standard bearer of the Ninth Legion leapt forward – if the standard was captured by the Britons then the entire Legion would be disgraced.

When the Britons appeared in war chariots the Romans were startled, but after a hard struggle they won through to dry land. As the Cantii faded away the Roman cavalry should have given chase, but naval confusion meant they arrived late. Channel crossings haven't changed much!

The Cantii seemed inclined to abandon the struggle, but their hopes were raised when much of Caesar's fleet was damaged in a storm; a lot of equipment was lost. The Britons began a campaign of attrition, hoping to wear down the Romans without having to fight a pitched battle. It was a sensible policy.

Caesar established a firm base camp and sent out the Seventh Legion southwards towards the present settlement of Martin Mill, looking for corn to plunder. However, the Legion was ambushed by the Britons and severely tested by the war chariots again. This success made them too confident and they dropped their previous cautious policy in favour of more daring tactics; a frontal assault on Caesar's camp soon proved a fiasco for them. Caesar was able to regroup and retire to Gaul, feeling that his punitive expedition had been a success. The Senate certainly agreed, for they voted a 20 day celebration.

Caesar decided to repeat the venture the following year and this time amassed 600 new ships, five legions and 2,000 cavalry. He was able to make an unopposed landing near present-day Walmer, and by 7th July 54BC, 30,000 Roman soldiers were on the soil of the Cantii.

The Romans marched quickly inland by night, advancing twelve miles towards Thannington and hoping to surprise the Cantii by the pace of their movements. The Britons chose to put up a fight at a ford across the Stour, but the Roman cavalry pushed them back to the hills beyond.

The Cantii retired to their hillfort at Bigbury. Though its timber defences may have been adequate protection during tribal squabbles, it proved no obstacle for the Romans who captured it easily – only to find that the Cantii chiefs had already fled!

But disaster struck Caesar on the night of 8th–9th July. A gale blew up and wreaked havoc amidst his anchored fleet – 40 ships were destroyed and many others badly damaged. This setback did not destroy Caesar's determination, though it encouraged the Cantii to seek help from Caswallon or 'Cassivellaunus', a much more important chief based at a site close to present-day Wheathampstead in Hertfordshire.

Caesar was not to be intimidated and advanced deeper into Kent, though he was harried at all turns by the Britons who operated a 'scorched earth' policy in advance of his movements. The Romans crossed the Medway near Rochester and the Thames near Brentford; they were storming the gates of Caswallon's base when he decided to ask for peace. Caesar demanded cattle and slaves as the price, then withdrew.

In the meantime the base camp near Walmer had again been attacked by the Cantii, but without success. Caesar withdrew to Gaul and ceased to play a part in Kent history, for he never returned.

Instead he went back to Rome where he became involved in endless political turmoil and conflict. It was this, of course, that led to his assassination in 44BC; perhaps he would have been better advised to stay in Kent!

CHRISTOPHER MARLOWE
DRAMATIST AND SPY

C HRISTOPHER Marlowe's short life was tempestuous and controversial, yet in his 28 years he wrote several works which have ensured his place in the pantheon of English literature. Indeed, many critics have said that only his bizarre and mysterious murder prevented him from becoming the greatest dramatist in English history – superior even to Shakespeare.

Marlowe was born in Canterbury in 1564, the son of a prosperous man who has been variously described as a shoemaker, victualler and clerk. Marlowe's intelligence proved the foundation of his success when, after a short spell at King's School in Canterbury, he won a place at Corpus Christi College in Cambridge. Arriving there in 1580 he soon developed an interest in the classics which coloured much of his later poetry. In 1581 he won a scholarship.

He passed his first degree without too much difficulty, but when it came to the awarding of an MA in 1587 he encountered problems. The University authorities considered that he had been away too often and a trip to Rheims had given rise to rumours that he might turn Catholic. Marlowe was defended by a letter from the Privy Council informing the University that he had been away 'on matters touching the benefit of this country.' Many have assumed from this that Marlowe had been working as an intelli-

A 19th century drawing of Butchery Lane in the old city of Canterbury. Narrow streets and alleys such as this were home to the young Christopher Marlowe.

gence agent for Thomas Walsingham of Chislehurst, who was employed by Queen Elizabeth.

Some have thought that Marlowe spent some time in the Army after Cambridge, but this seems unlikely as he was soon involved in drama. He became attached to the Earl of Nottingham's company.

Marlowe had time for other activities as well. He was often at Scadbury, near Chislehurst, to visit Walsingham and may have worked for him as a double agent – hence the suspicion of him turning Catholic. He was also a friend of Sir Walter Raleigh, and involved with him in a dubious group called the 'School of the Night'. Marlowe was greatly interested in atheism and black magic, though Sir Walter was rather more cautious.

Marlowe's first important play was *Tamburlaine the Great*, though early editions do not bear his name. It was probably written in 1587, and made great use of blank verse. The content, though, questioned the existence of God and thereby won Marlowe many enemies.

In about 1588 Marlowe wrote *Faustus*, a play which was perhaps inspired by his own dabbling with the occult. According to one legend, the Devil himself appeared onstage during a performance of the play at the Belsavage Playhouse.

Marlowe found it hard to avoid trouble. In October 1588 the authorities were pursuing him about an unknown matter and in 1589 he was involved in a street brawl at Canterbury in which a man died. In 1592 he was again involved in a fight at Canterbury.

He wrote *The Jew of Malta* in about 1590 and *Edward II* soon afterwards. Some of the works thought to be by Shakespeare have also been ascribed at least in part to Marlowe – notably *The Taming of the Shrew* and *Titus Andronicus*. In 1592 the dramatic part of Marlowe's career suffered an interruption when all theatres were closed because of plague and he seems to have occupied himself in the interim by writing *Hero and Leander*, an epic poem which he never finished.

In 1592 Marlowe may well have been an active secret agent again, carrying letters from France for Sir Robert Cecil. His background, however, perhaps made him an unsuitable choice for a spy.

In 1591 he had begun sharing rooms with another dramatist, Thomas Kyd. On 12th May 1593 their rooms were ransacked and Kyd was arrested on a charge of treason. At the same time a search was made of the rooms and a number of atheistic papers were discovered. Kyd said they belonged to Marlowe and on 18th May a warrant for his arrest was issued.

Marlowe was at Chislehurst at the time but was ordered to report to the Privy Council each day – he could have been flung into prison immediately. An informer, Robert Baines, accused Marlowe of blasphemy, treason and homosexuality. An associate of Marlowe's, Richard Strange, was also arrested.

Marlowe died in the middle of his legal troubles, in circumstances which have stirred debate ever since. At the very least his death was highly unusual. The official story was that Marlowe was stabbed to death on 30th May 1593 at a beer house in Deptford run by Eleanor Bull. Apparently he had spent the day drinking and was in an upstairs room with three associates – Robert Poley, Nicholas Skeres and Ingram Frizer. A drunken argument is said to have developed, either about cards or about a 'lewde love', and Marlowe reached for his knife. Frizer reacted more quickly, and stabbed Marlowe in the eye – a blow which killed him almost immediately.

Several aspects of Marlowe's death are strange. Firstly, Frizer was pardoned for the crime on 28th June – an unusual event for a drunken murderer. Secondly, all those involved had 'secret service' links: Frizer was an associate of Sir Francis Walsingham (who had arranged many plots to benefit the Queen), whilst both Skeres and Poley had worked for the Government in 'cloak and dagger' exploits.

Thus it seems possible that Marlowe was murdered by his former associates in Government circles. It may be that he had once been useful as a spy but by 1593 was behaving in an increasingly unreliable and dangerous way; being an atheist in those times was a very unusual thing, and certain to attract attention. Was the killing of Marlowe an attempt to dispose of a problem?

HUBERT DE BURGH
EARL OF KENT

HUBERT de Burgh was a noble Baron of the medieval period, who was plunged into the strife that beset England during the reign of King John. In 1200 King John divorced his wife Isabella and sent Hubert de Burgh to Portugal to ask for the hand of a princess. The mission proved to be the first of a series of uncomfortable moments in the career of de Burgh – while he was in Portugal John got married to Isabella of Angouleme instead! Imagine explaining that to the prospective father-in-law.

King John rewarded de Burgh with the post of King's Chamberlain in 1201. But de Burgh was also a soldier and in 1204 distinguished himself by defending the castle of Chinon, in France, for a whole year against French troops. He finally had to abandon it and launched into a fierce battle against his enemies before being wounded and captured.

King John trusted de Burgh enough to make him an adviser at the time of Magna Carta, but the King continued to have a lot of difficulty controlling the other Barons. By 1215 England was a divided nation and some of the Barons invited Prince Louis of France to intervene, much to the disgust of de Burgh.

On 23rd May 1216 Louis landed near Sandwich, supported by

600 ships. He met no opposition and easily captured Rochester Castle, entering London on 2nd June. Within weeks the whole of southern England was in the hands of Louis – with one important exception.

De Burgh had also been appointed Lord Warden of the Cinque Ports and Constable of Dover Castle by King John, and he refused to surrender his charges to the foreign prince. Louis demanded that Dover Castle should be handed over, but de Burgh had prepared for a siege and was determined to hold out. Though his defenders only numbered about 140 knights and local people, de Burgh even rejected Louis' substantial bribes. One of the bribes would have given him Norfolk and Suffolk!

Louis brought in a 'siege engine' named the Evil Neighbour and gradually the castle was battered, but it was not until mid-October

Dover from the sea. In his role as Lord Warden of the Cinque Ports, Hubert de Burgh must have set sail with the Kentish fleet many times from here. (Author's collection)

that de Burgh finally emerged from it to negotiate a truce. By that time King John had had much valuable time in which to reorganise his defences, though he had little chance to enjoy this improvement since he died a few days after the end of the siege of Dover.

John was succeeded by his son, Henry III, who was still a child. The Earl of Pembroke was appointed Protector and de Burgh became High Justiciary. But in the summer of 1217 Prince Louis gathered together a new invasion fleet under Eustace the Monk, intending to attack Kent again. De Burgh gathered the forces of the Cinque Ports and it was at this time that he is credited with calling Dover Castle the 'key of England'. The Kentish men took their fleet out under de Burgh's leadership on 24th August and defeated the French in a battle off the North Foreland. Eustace was beheaded. On 11th September 1217 the Treaty of Lambeth was signed and the French abandoned their attempt at conquest, finally leaving Kent in peace.

In 1219 Pembroke died so de Burgh became a co-Regent with Peter de Roches, the Bishop of Winchester. When the young king reached the age of 16, de Burgh gave up control of the Tower of London and Dover Castle to him. In February 1227 de Burgh was made Earl of Kent. This was the peak of his career, for his later years were sadly troubled.

De Burgh had already made himself unpopular with the people of London. In 1222 a riot had started, led by a prominent citizen. De Burgh had made many arrests, hanged the leader, and had a number of other prisoners mutilated. Some people also disliked his choice of a third wife – Isabella, formerly the wife of King John.

In 1229 Henry III gave Hubert de Burgh the task of trying to regain some of the lands he had lost in Gascony. The expedition was a fiasco from the very start, with only half the number of ships required being provided. De Burgh received most of the blame for this setback.

In 1231 he fell out with the Archbishop of Canterbury. De Burgh controlled the town and castle of Tonbridge, which the Archbishop claimed by a tradition going back to Becket. The

Archbishop also criticised de Burgh for marrying again to Margaret, whom he considered to be too closely related to Isabella.

On 29th July 1232 de Burgh was dismissed by Henry and accused of corruption. Fearing for his life, he fled to Merton Abbey in Surrey. Such was London's hatred of him that the Lord Mayor led a march of 20,000 citizens to Merton with the intention of bringing him back 'dead or alive'. This would have been an undignified end for an Earl of Kent, but Henry intervened just in time to save de Burgh's life.

Soon afterwards de Burgh announced that he intended going to Scotland, but instead he turned towards Essex in the hope of reaching his wife, who was staying a little further north at Bury St Edmunds. De Burgh stopped at the Bishop of Norwich's house in Brentwood, where Henry III attempted to have him arrested. De Burgh fled into the chapel and claimed sanctuary, but was dragged

Dover castle and beach, a peaceful setting for the Victorian holidaymakers in this 19th century sketch, was an embattled place in 1216 when Hubert de Burgh held the castle against Prince Louis of France.

out naked, clutching the cross from the altar in one hand and sanctified bread in the other.

A local blacksmith was ordered to make fetters for him, but refused to fix them to so noble a warrior. However the Bishop of London had by this time heard of the invasion of sanctuary and threatened to excommunicate everyone involved unless de Burgh was allowed to return to the Bishop's house. Henry's soldiers consented and de Burgh returned, only this time they surrounded the house with trenches and starved him out.

De Burgh spent some time in the Tower of London and was also imprisoned at Devizes Castle, from which he again escaped to a church. The King's mind had been poisoned against him by the Bishop of Winchester but he found a defender in the Bishop of Salisbury, and the Bishop of Winchester was removed in 1234.

Hubert de Burgh, defender of Dover Castle and Earl of Kent, died in 1243.

SIR SAMUEL MORTON PETO
RAILWAY KING

MANY thousands of Kent people owe a debt to Sir Morton Peto, whose labours during the mid 19th century make it possible today to live deep in Kent and yet work in London. Peto was a railway contractor and speculator who rose to power and prominence in the years between the Railway Mania of the 1840s and 'Black Friday' in 1866. He tended, however, to be associated with impecunious concerns such as the London, Chatham & Dover Railway, a highly unreliable concern with which his fate became hopelessly entwined.

Samuel Morton Peto (he was always called by his second name) was born at Whitmore House, Woking. As a youth he was apprenticed to his Uncle Henry as a builder. Though the young Peto soon showed a talent for drawing and draughtsmanship, he was also expected to learn the building trade from the bottom up: he learnt carpentry and bricklaying, becoming so proficient at the latter that he could lay 800 bricks a day. He finished his apprenticeship in 1830, when he inherited his uncle's business jointly with his cousin Thomas Grissell.

Grissell & Peto became a dynamic partnership that did much to alter the face of London between 1830 and 1847. The uncertainty of the post-Napoleonic War years was giving way to prosperity, and there was much for builders to do. Their first major contract was to complete the Hungerford Market in 1832–3 for £42,400, a contract won in open competition, unlike many of Peto's later railway contracts. The partners then went on to build a series of the clubhouses which were then becoming fashionable; the 'Oxford & Cambridge', the 'Reform' and the 'Conservative' were all built by Grissell & Peto. Branching out a little, they built Nelson's Column and the Lyceum, St James and the Olympic theatres.

By the early 1840s railway contracts were starting to offer lucrative possibilities and Peto was not slow to spot that here was a major chance for expansion. He was involved with the building of Curzon Street station in Birmingham, but his first true railway contract came with the construction of a section of the Great Western Railway between Hanwell and Langley in 1840.

Sir Morton Peto built the railway across the Thames at Blackfriars that linked Kent to the North via Farringdon. This scene shows the construction of the line in 1864 and reveals the enormous scale of the undertaking. (Author's collection)

Railway work in East Anglia soon followed and Peto constructed the first railway to Lowestoft. There he bought the harbour and set about using his own men to turn it into a premier East Coast port. He bought a large mansion nearby at Somerleyton, and transformed it into a palace, including houses for the estate workers and a new Anglican church, though he himself was a Baptist. Some reckoned that Peto fancied himself as 'King' of Lowestoft, and an anonymous booklet was published which satirised the town as 'Petovia'. Whilst at Lowestoft, Peto formed connections with an East Anglian banking family named Gurney; they were to have a role in his downfall.

In Kent, Peto became involved with building the section of the South Eastern Railway through Folkestone. The course of the line here was a difficult one, and Peto constructed the beautiful Foord viaduct which was first crossed by an official train on 14th November 1843. A treat was laid on for the navvies.

1846 saw a rearrangement of Peto's business affairs. On the Folkestone contract he had begun to work with Edward Ladd Betts and it was decided that the two men would form a new partnership. Grissell was to concentrate on buildings, leaving the Peto & Betts partnership to construct railways. Betts (1815–1872) had already established himself as a railway contractor on the South Eastern line in Kent, and also built the line from Paddock Wood to Maidstone. His arrangement with Peto brought him great success, and he rose to become High Sheriff of Kent, building for himself a mansion at Preston Hall near Maidstone. Like Peto, though, Betts was broken by financial disaster and died at Aswan in Egypt whilst trying to rebuild his health.

With Betts, Peto built railways throughout England and the world. The people of Argentina, Russia, Algeria and Norway still owe a debt of gratitude to their partnership.

The two men also teamed up with another contractor, Thomas Brassey, to build railways in Australia, Canada, Denmark, Germany and France. Then, with Thomas Crampton, born at Broadstairs in 1816, they built railways in Russia, and became deeply embroiled in the affairs of the London, Chatham & Dover Railway.

If Peto had been content to simply build railways to contract, he might never have experienced disaster. Instead he took the view that if only more railways could be built, then he could make more money! As early as 1845 he began to accept shares instead of hard cash in order to encourage such schemes, generally taking the shares at a severe discount and getting the contract to build the line without competition.

During the mid 1850s and early 1860s, the East Kent Railway, latterly the London, Chatham & Dover Railway, fell into Peto's clutches. He transformed it from a struggling local line connecting Strood and Canterbury into a powerful main line from the heart of London to Dover. He also encouraged the company to invest millions of pounds in building lines through London to Blackfriars and Farringdon. He was awarded the contract, worth £5.9 million, without it being put out to tender; he also lent the LCDR money with which to pay himself, at 14½% interest!

The mid 1850s were the time when Peto became a national figure. He was elected MP for Norwich in 1847, and in 1851 rescued the Great Exhibition from disaster by helping in the construction of the Crystal Palace. In Parliament he sponsored a Bill dealing with religious property laws that became known as 'Peto's Act'.

In 1854 war broke out in the Crimea and the British Army had severe problems with transportation – as with virtually everything else in a campaign characterised by the ineptness of the senior officers. Peto arranged for some navvies to be sent to the Crimea to build a railway from Balaclava to the battlefield. A contract was arranged but he refused to accept any commission or profit on it. However, as it was a contract with the Government he had to resign his seat in Parliament. In compensation he was created a baronet in 1855.

Peto demanded high moral standards on his sites. He supported the Truck Acts, which forbade the payment of wages in 'tokens' that could only be redeemed at highly-priced contractors' shops, ran sick clubs for the workmen and imposed strict controls on alcohol. He took legal action against any of his sub-contractors who attempted to set up their own 'tommy shops' in breach of the Truck Acts and provided reading rooms so the navvies could put their spare time to good use. It was said that if Peto was the contractor, 'the gin shops were left deserted and the schools were full.'

But his good Baptist principles did not extend to all areas of Peto's life, and his business style was cruelly exposed by the collapse of a major London banking firm on 'Black Friday', 11th May 1866. Overend, Gurney & Co had lent too much on too little security, and they brought down Peto & Betts with them. The debts of the railway contractors were reckoned to be in the order of £4 million.

'Navvies' at work on the Metropolitan Extension Railway at Smithfield. Sir Morton Peto treated his workforce well. It was said that if he was the contractor, 'the gin shops were left deserted and the schools were full'!

The *Economist* expected Peto to 'emerge from the cloud a very rich man still, and with a character for honour beyond the reach of any question.' He clung on to his seat in Parliament, telling his Bristol constituents that he still possessed one 'priceless jewel' which was 'a conscious feeling of his own integrity.' Gladstone, a political friend, described Peto as 'a man who has attained a high position in this country by the exercise of rare talents and has adorned that position by his great virtues'.

But, exactly two years after 'Black Friday', the reckoning came when he was declared personally bankrupt. Peto sold all his possessions and his houses, then attempted to start again with a new railway contract in Cornwall. It ended in another failure.

He was a broken man and retired to Blackhurst, on the outskirts of Tunbridge Wells. There he died on 13th November 1889, leaving seven sons and seven daughters. He is buried beside his wife in the beautiful country churchyard at Pembury, where a new lychgate was erected as a memorial.

But Peto's real memorial is in the railway system of Kent, which owes much to his energies. Almost a hundred years after his death, one of his greatest projects was reborn – the railway from Blackfriars to Farringdon that he built and which largely ruined the finances of the LCDR. Reopened to passengers in 1988, it is a living testament to the effect that this extraordinary man has had on the daily lives of thousands of Kent commuters.

SAINT AUGUSTINE
MISSIONARY OF CHRIST

HEN Hengist and Horsa landed at Ebbsfleet in AD 449, few could have believed that it would be a descendant of the fiercely-pagan Hengist who would establish Christianity as the official religion of Kent. Hengist and his cohorts had come to Kent at the invitation of Vortigern, who was badly in need of military help in his endless military struggles.

Hengist laid claim to the title 'King of Kent', not being content with the Isle of Thanet which he had been offered. However, this title was rightfully claimed by his descendant Ethelbert, born in AD 545. At the age of about 15 Ethelbert became King of Kent and then made a suitable royal marriage to Bertha, the daughter of King Charibert of France. Bertha brought her Christian chaplain, Luidhard, and he was allowed to build a chapel in Canterbury. Ethelbert was tolerant towards his wife's religion, but the old pagan ways continued to dominate both him and Kent. Luidhard seems to have made little impact on the pagan city of Canterbury.

The man usually credited with the initiative in organising a mission to England was Gregory, later to become Pope. According to ancient legend it was about the year AD 585 when Gregory saw some young slaves being led through the streets of Rome. Their

Saint Augustine's Gateway at Canterbury.

clear skins and blonde hair impressed him – he was used to the darker Roman complexion. Gregory asked who the youths were. 'They are Angles,' he was told; 'Surely not Angles, but Angels,' he is said to have replied.

Whatever the truth of the legend it was Gregory who instructed Augustine to form a mission to the land of the Angles in AD 596. But Augustine proved to be rather faint-hearted, and had hardly left Italy when rumours about the English began to terrify him. They were, he was told, utterly ferocious and barbaric. Augustine crept back to Rome hoping for permission to abandon his task, but Gregory was inflexible. Augustine had to go.

Thus it was that in AD 596 Augustine landed at Ebbsfleet. Ethelbert had heard of his approach, but decided to keep the new missionary at a safe distance from Canterbury. He met Augustine at Ebbsfleet, prepared to give him at least a fair hearing on one condition – they must meet out in the open since Ethelbert feared Augustine might have magic powers which could be more dangerous in an enclosed space! Augustine unpacked his most impressive regalia for the occasion – a huge silver cross and a painting of Christ.

After listening to Augustine's sermon, Ethelbert gave him permission to go to Canterbury via Richborough. The newly-arrived Christians were allowed to worship at St Martin's chapel, soon creating a good impression of themselves. Ethelbert was struck by the pure lives and miracles of the Christians, and in AD 597 was converted. On 2nd June Ethelbert was baptised and his tribe followed; Augustine is said to have baptised 10,000 of them!

After this important success Augustine went to Arles in France and was consecrated Archbishop. Thus he had the authority to begin building a Church in England. The Pope sent him a string of helpers – Mellitus, Justus, Paulinus, Rufinianus – and some holy relics as well.

Augustine laid plans for the building of a monastery beside the Roman road into Canterbury, intending it to be his burial place. The first Abbot was a man named Peter, who drowned near

The landing of Saint Augustine at Ebbsfleet in AD 596. He was to become the first Archbishop of Canterbury.

Ambleteuse when on a journey into France. Disrespectful local people threw Peter's body into a mean pauper's grave, but each night afterwards a heavenly light shone on the spot until the Frenchmen buried Peter properly in Boulogne.

Other missionaries had been at work in more northern parts of England and Augustine hoped to create a united English Church by joining forces with them. However, when he went to meet the other leaders some disputes developed. Augustine decided to re-solve the question of authority by getting his opponents to pray for a blind man – whoever's prayer healed him would be the future leader. Of course it was Augustine who succeeded!

A hermit is said to have advised the other leaders to only follow Augustine if he remained humble – the test being to see if he stood when others entered the room. Accounts vary as to whether he did or not. The other British Christians so troubled Augustine that he revealed a prophecy to them – they would soon be massacred by pagans. When Gregory heard of miracles attributed to Augustine, he wrote to warn him of the dangers of vanity – so perhaps he had the same opinion as the hermit.

The exact date of Augustine's death is usually said to be 26th May, but the year has variously been claimed as AD 604 or AD 605. One of his last acts was to consecrate Justus and Mellitus as Bishops of Rochester and London respectively.

Augustine has been held in high honour ever since. At the second Council of Cloveshoe (Cliffe-at-Hoo) in AD 747 his annual festival was declared a public holiday. In 1221 his head was put in a rich shrine of gold and precious stones, while his other bones were laid to rest in a marble tomb. Though his claim to be the Father of English Christianity may be debatable, he was certainly the founder of the religion in Kent and the first Archbishop of Canterbury.

Sir John Oldcastle
Martyr or Fool?

S IR John Oldcastle, involved in one of the most extraordinary incidents in the history of Cooling Castle, has been described in an alarmingly wide variety of ways. Claims made about him include that he was the father of Protestantism in Kent, that he was Elijah, and that he was the inspiration for Shakespeare's Falstaff. But who was he really?

He was born in about 1378, probably in Herefordshire where his family owned land. In 1401 he was commanding a castle at Builth in the Welsh Marches, and in 1404 he became MP for Hereford. From 1406 he was also Sheriff of Hereford. All these posts he combined with various other military duties.

His association with Kent began in 1409 when he married Joan, Lady Cobham. With this marriage he gained control of Cobham Manor and Cooling Castle. Shortly afterwards he became a Baron.

From about 1411 Oldcastle was often in the company of the Prince of Wales, the future Henry V, and saw action in France. In this role he has appeared in many dramas, often cast unfairly as 'the aged counsellor to the youthful sin'. In fact Oldcastle was not a great deal older than Henry; the mistake may be due to his name. Nor was he unusually guilty of 'gluttony, covetousness and lechery'. The Falstaff image is also not matched by his eventual fate.

In about 1410 Oldcastle became influenced by the Lollards, a group of religious reformers critical of the Catholic Church. Oldcastle allowed the churches on his manorial estates to become centres of Lollardy but in 1410 the churches of Hoo, Halstow and Cooling were placed under a Church edict due to the unauthorised preaching there of 'Sir John the Chaplain' – presumably Oldcastle himself.

Oldcastle was no doubt helped by his friendship with Henry. Some said that he even tried to convert the young Prince to his views. Henry became King in 1413 and Oldcastle got into more trouble almost immediately.

In March 1413 he was in difficulties for celebrating the mass with an unlicensed priest. Then in June a shop in Paternoster Row, London, was raided and 'dangerous tracts' found there. The shopkeeper said they belonged to Oldcastle, who tried to excuse himself on the grounds that he'd only read two pages of them. In August 1413 he was summoned to Windsor to see the King, but a furious row developed and he left at speed for Cooling, where he barricaded himself inside the castle.

Thomas Arundel, the Archbishop, accused Oldcastle of heresy and issued a summons. This had to be delivered to the named offender in person, but when the messenger reached Cooling he was refused entry. The summons for heresy was therefore pinned to the door of Rochester cathedral on 5th September 1413, from where it was twice torn down by Oldcastle's supporters. Oldcastle failed to meet the Archbishop at Leeds Castle on 11th September as requested, and so was excommunicated. A rumour spread that he had denounced the Pope as Antichrist.

Oldcastle was arrested eventually and tried for heresy in London on 23rd September. The two key issues were Sir Thomas' attitude to transubstantiation (whether the bread used in the mass was actually converted into the body of Christ) and the role of confession to a priest. On 25th September he was declared a heretic and

The south entrance at Cooling castle, as it looked in the 1880s. Here Sir John Oldcastle shut the gates to prevent service of his writ for heresy and later, a pitched battle was fought during the Wyatt rebellion. (Author's collection)

given 40 days to recant, after which he would be executed. Meanwhile he was thrown into the Tower.

Oldcastle promised to recant and so his chains were removed, but this only allowed him to escape from the Tower. Some said he achieved this with the help of the Devil himself! For a while Oldcastle hid in the London house of a parchment-maker, for which the man was executed in 1416.

Rumours spread of a Lollard conspiracy led by Sir Thomas, which apparently intended to capture the King at Eltham on 6th January 1414. A gathering of Lollards outside London was dispersed and 1,000 marks offered as a reward for the capture of Oldcastle. He was declared an outlaw – a sad fate for Kent's first Lord Cobham.

By 1415 he was back in his old haunts on the Welsh borders,

and narrowly evaded capture in Malvern. The following year a supporter of his was blamed for an attempt to kill Henry V at Kenilworth. Oldcastle was said to be plotting with the Scots, then he was nearly caught at St Albans. A book of his was found in whch the name of the Virgin Mary had been erased wherever it occurred!

In 1417 Sir Thomas was caught at last, whilst trying to hide in the Welsh Marches. There was a desperate struggle in which several men were killed. One story was that a woman broke his leg with a stool during the melee. On 14th December 1417 he was condemned by Parliament as a traitor and heretic, and the next day he was hanged and burnt at St Giles' Fields.

Stories that he was Elijah and would rise again on the third day proved false, but his fame rose again 200 years later in a series of Elizabethan plays about him, written in 1600 and 1601. It is said that Shakespeare intended originally to use his name in *Henry IV* but that the Lord Cobham at the time objected – though the name may have been used in some performances before being altered to Falstaff. Oldcastle, though, is best remembered as a deeply religious man who died for his beliefs rather than as the corrupt and worldly Falstaff.

JACK CADE'S REVOLT

WRITING over a hundred years after Cade's death, Shakespeare described him as 'a headstrong Kentishman'. He was certainly a man of strong temperament but his career as a rebel brought only sadness to Kent, ending in what became known as the 'harvest of heads'.

Cade's first career seems to have been as a soldier, taking part in the Duke of York's campaigns in Ireland during the mid-1400s. However he seems to have got into trouble for he was accused of murder and had to flee abroad.

Cade returned to England under the name of 'Aylmer' and took up residence near Canterbury, probably at Wye, earning a living as a physician. This says a lot about the standards of medical practice at the time. He married a girl from Tonbridge.

In 1450 Cade emerged as the leader of a revolt by Kent men, though he claimed to be loyal to Henry VI. The revolt broke out around Ashford and soon gained support from other Kent towns. Hythe is said to have sent Cade a porpoise as a token of its support.

Cade's grievances were defined in the list of 15 'Articles of Complaint' and five 'Articles of Request' that he sent to Henry VI. These were formulated after Cade had gathered together a force of 20,000 men and marched to Blackheath — where he defeated forces led by Stafford.

Cade had a number of complaints to make, though he felt that many were the fault of the King's advisers rather than the King himself. Perhaps the most unlikely worry he had was that Kent was going to be turned into a wild forest, presumably as a hunting ground for the high and mighty. Many of the complaints had to do with taxation – that the King used the money improperly, that people's goods were taken for the King's personal use, and that extortion was practiced by the collectors.

Some of the complaints were quite practical. The West Kent men among Cade's rebels complained that the County Sessions were held too far east and requested that Kent be split into two.

Having camped out at Blackheath the rebels stormed London Bridge and forced their way into the City, taking over Smithfield. They beheaded Lord Say and the High Sheriff of Kent, Sir William Cromer, at Mile End. Then on 6th July 1450 a truce was declared while the complaints were discussed.

The Chancellor, Cardinal Kemp, issued a pardon for all of the rebels and many began to drift home. Cade arranged for the plunder he had collected to be sent back to Rochester on a barge – so he had clearly done very well out of the venture!

However, Cade's pardon was made out in the name of Mortimer, one of his aliases. Thus it was invalid – especially as a reward of 1,000 marks had now been placed on him, 'quick or dead'. He fled from London, pausing only to stir up new revolts at Dartford and Rochester. Eventually he went to Queenborough, where the Mayor was among his supporters, but failed to capture the castle there.

Alexander Iden, the new Sheriff of Kent, began a search for the fugitive. Cade's supporters had mostly been satisfied with the free pardons and had deserted him. Iden traced Cade to Heathfield in Sussex where he was captured and killed. On 16th July his body was beheaded and quartered. The four parts were sent to Blackheath, Norwich, Salisbury and Gloucester while the head was put up on London Bridge.

Kemp then went to Rochester to take charge of Cade's loot. £40 of it was given to the city to repair its east gate.

A commission was sent to Kent to try Cade's followers but further trouble broke out, led by William Parmynter of Faversham and also a John Smith. The Government became much tougher and at Christmas 1450 executed 29 Kent people, including eight at Canterbury. This became known as the 'harvest of heads'.

Parmynter's rebellion was not very successful and on 23rd February 1451 200 of his supporters met Henry VI at Blackheath. They provided a sorry contrast to Cade's passage past the same spot as they knelt half-naked before the King, with ropes round their necks, to beg for mercy.

Anne Boleyn
Queen of England

THE name of Anne Boleyn is closely associated with Hever Castle, but stories that she was born there or lived there while Henry was wooing her are false. The Kent castle did, however, play a key role in her story.

Hever Castle was built by Geoffrey Boleyn, Lord Mayor of London in 1457–8, but the Boleyns also owned estates in Norfolk and it was there that Anne was born. Her father, Thomas, was a courtier.

Anne was born in about 1501 and she had an older sister called Mary. In 1513 Anne was sent abroad as maid of honour to Margaret of Austria, who was then ruling the Netherlands. This introduced her to the world of courtlife and diplomacy, for she was present at the great diplomatic meetings at Lille and Tournai. When Anne moved to France she was able to take part in Henry VIII's great meeting with the French king at the 'Field of the Cloth of Gold' – an event which virtually all the Boleyn family attended.

In 1521 she returned to England to find the court alive with rumours involving the young King Henry and members of her own family. It was common knowledge that Anne's sister, Mary, had been the King's mistress until being married off in 1520. Years later some Catholics were to allege that Anne's mother had also been Henry's mistress and that Anne was actually his daughter – but as Henry himself was only born in 1490 this would have credited him with a rather unusual rate of development.

Back in England, Anne soon became involved in romances herself. A possible marriage with James Butler was stopped by the intervention of Wolsey, the King's most trusted adviser. Anne compensated by having flirtations with Henry Percy and Sir Thomas Wyatt. Henry instructed Wolsey to stop marriage plans between Anne and Percy, and Percy was hurriedly married off. He was later forced to serve as one of the jury that sentenced her to death – an experience from which he never recovered.

Thomas Wyatt was a Kent nobleman and a distinguished poet. Living at Allington Castle, he would have been well-known to the Boleyn family at Hever, and it is said that several of his love poems were inspired by Anne. 'I would gladly yield to be tied forever with the knot of her love,' he wrote.

Stories about the relationship between Anne and Wyatt multiplied. She was apparently sent back to Hever to 'cool off' from her love affairs, but one story claimed that Wyatt made midnight visits to her room at Hever – climbing in through the window. Another claims that when he scrambled in, out of breath, he found her already waiting – for another man! Wyatt was arrested in 1536 along with other men said to have been her lovers, but he was later released.

In 1524 Henry's relationship with Catherine of Aragon began to deteriorate and he may have begun his pursuit of Anne in 1526. In September 1527 he began his series of requests for a divorce. The Pope was unobliging, though Henry would not have been the first King to be granted a divorce. Despite her reputation as a loose woman, it seems that Anne steadfastly clung to the view that Henry should not enjoy a physical relationship with her until she was his wife.

Thus the romance was already in progress when Anne was sent out to Hever again in June 1528. This was because one of her ladies had developed an illness called 'the sweat' and Anne was

Hever castle, built by Geoffrey Boleyn, Lord mayor of London 1457–8.

put into quarantine. She soon caught the disease herself, but recovered and returned quickly to London.

In September 1528 Anne was again sent back to Hever. Henry was expecting a visit from Cardinal Campeggio, the Papal Legate, and wished to put on a display of proper relationships. Whilst Anne was at Hever all the messengers to and from Rome were instructed to call in there to keep her informed. In November, though, Henry began to despair of ever getting the divorce and rushed to Hever to see Anne. She gave him the same answer as always – no marriage, no marital relations! Henry moved her back to London for Christmas.

A stalemate then developed on both fronts. Henry made no progress with Anne and none with the Pope either. The greatest sufferer was Wolsey, whose position was undermined by Anne in revenge for his thwarting her earlier romances.

On 1st September 1532 Henry ennobled Anne as Marchioness

of Pembroke. They went to Calais shortly afterwards and it seems that the relationship was consummated at about this time. Henry and Anne were married secretly on 25th January 1533 and she was crowned Queen on 1st June – events which had an enormous impact on the religious life of the country because of the break with the Catholic Church which this demanded. Anne's daughter, Elizabeth, was born on 7th September 1533.

Anne was an object of hatred for many Catholics. Some called her unkind names such as 'goggle-eyed whore', the 'Nun of Kent' prophesied against her, and many said she was a witch. Physical descriptions of her encouraged these prejudices, such as this one by a Catholic propagandist:

> 'Anne Boleyn was rather tall of stature, with black hair and an oval face of sallow complexion, as if troubled with jaundice. She had a projecting tooth under the upper lip, and on her right hand, six fingers. There was a large wen under her chin, and therefore to hide its ugliness, she wore a high dress covering her throat.'

Was this really the same woman that Henry went to so much trouble to marry?

Anne's era as Henry's favourite woman was a short one. In January 1536 she lost the baby she was expecting, a boy, and Henry became interested in Jane Seymour. The moves to depose Anne were led by Thomas Cromwell, once Wolsey's henchman. Anne's downfall was plotted to take advantage of her reputation as a loose woman and on 30th April 1536 Mark Smeton was arrested for adultery with her. Smeton was a musician and in his alleged confession said that a secret code between him and Anne meant that whenever she asked for marmalade it meant she required his services.

Anne was beheaded along with four of her supposed lovers, in a very hastily arranged session at the Tower. She at least had the dignity of her own coffin; the bodies of her 'lovers' were packed in two at a time.

THE NUNS OF HIGHAM

LOWER Higham today is a tiny hamlet where even the pub has closed down. It has the atmosphere of a remote place, over which the mists and the rain of the Thames estuary roll relentlessly. The casual visitor would be hard-pressed to find any signs of the old Higham Priory there, nor remains of the causeway the nuns were meant to maintain across the marshes and down to the river Thames. Nor would the visitor imagine that such a hamlet was once a 'hotbed' of scandal.

Higham Priory was never large, but by 1501 it had declined from having about 16 nuns to only three or four. When Prioress Elizabeth Bradforth resigned that year, there were only two suitable candidates to replace her; Agnes Swayne was appointed.

In May 1508 Edward Steroper (or 'Sharpe') was instituted as vicar of Higham and rumours about the nuns began to circulate. John James, who was employed as a servant, later gave evidence that the Priory was often visited by 'lascivious persons', most of whom were priests and meant to be celibate like the nuns. The nuns also began to neglect their duties and failed to go to mass or give alms to the poor.

James found the Priory buildings to be falling down and was ordered by the Bishop of Rochester to repair them. However Priory funds were so depleted that it could not be done.

According to James, two nuns – Elizabeth Penny and Godliva

Lawrence – actually had babies within the Priory walls, with Steroper being reputedly the father of both children. This tale was corroborated by Eleanor Smyth of Cliffe, who was midwife at the birth of Penny's child. It was a boy, and Smyth took him to Cliffe to live but he died while still young.

Local stories about the immorality of the nuns continued to circulate and soon the Bishop of Rochester got to hear about them. On 2nd October 1512 he warned Steroper not to spend so much time with a nun called Lady Anchoreta Ungethorpe, it being alleged that he had met her in his room 'secretly'. Three weeks later Steroper had to be warned again, and this time he resigned.

Fisher, the Bishop of Rochester, decided that the nuns needed more spiritual sustenance and appointed John Standenought to celebrate mass at the Priory during 1512. Standenought was able to confirm the rumours about childbirth at the Priory.

In April 1513 John Parker was appointed to replace Steroper. In July the nuns petitioned the Bishop for permission to build a higher wall around the Priory as this would increase their 'virtue'. No doubt they hoped that this symbolic rejection of the world would improve their reputations, but the cynics probably thought they just wanted to keep their secrets hidden!

Anchoreta Ungethorpe was appointed Prioress in 1514, by which time there were only three nuns at Higham to choose from. The morals of the Priory seemed to improve until in 1519 Fisher received complaints from the other nuns about Anchoreta. They alleged that she was using the Priory's money to pay off her sister's debts.

Fisher sequestrated the Priory's funds and made a formal enquiry into its affairs. He was not pleased with its record and dissolved it in December 1521, the nuns being sent to stricter priories elsewhere, including Canterbury. Fisher used the remaining funds to help St John's College, Cambridge.

GENERAL JAMES WOLFE

'The world could not expect more of him than he thought himself capable of performing' – Horace Walpole

I N 1726 a boy was born at the vicarage in Westerham. Though his father was in the Army, few in the quiet country town could have expected the new child's name to become famous in every household across the land because of his military genius and tragic demise. For in his day James Wolfe became as much a hero as Lord Nelson and, in a way which seemed typical of British heroes in old-fashioned schoolbooks, contrived to die at his moment of greatest triumph.

James Wolfe's father rose to become a Major-General and his family lived in Westerham at a house called 'Spiers', later renamed 'Quebec House'. When he was eleven the family moved to Greenwich and the young lad was imbued with the military spirit. At 13 he volunteered to go with his father to Carthagena in Spain, but illness prevented this. One of his schoolfriends was Jack Jervis, who later became an admiral and was ennobled as Lord St Vincent.

Young James still had the chance to visit Westerham and was playing there with a friend when a messenger arrived to say that he had been awarded a commission in the Army: James was 14.

By 1742 he was in the 12th Regiment of Foot and carried their colours in the review at Blackheath. He soon gained experience of conflict in the campaign against the French at Dettingen. During this campaign his brother Edward, also in the Army, died of 'consumption'.

Wolfe then transferred to the 4th Regiment of Foot and was involved in the struggle against the Scottish Jacobites under Bonnie Prince Charlie. He was promoted to Major and took part in the last battle fought on the British mainland, at Culloden in 1745. A story is told that the commander of the Government forces, the Duke of Cumberland, ordered Wolfe to shoot a wounded prisoner; Cumberland was often referred to as 'Butcher'. Wolfe is said to have refused, saying, 'My commission is at Your Royal Highness' disposal, but I cannot consent to become an executioner.'

Back in Europe, Wolfe was wounded at the Battle of Laffeldt. He was also wounded in love, for while in London in 1747–8 he fell in love with Elizabeth Lawson. Wolfe's own parents opposed the match as they felt he was still too poor to support a wife, but

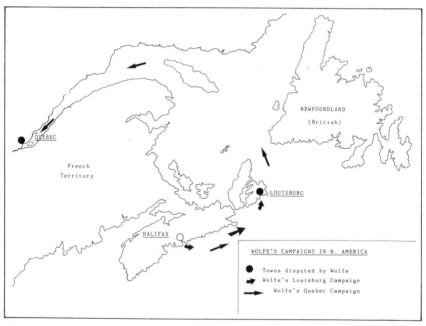

Map of North America, showing the progress of General James Wolfe's campaigns against the French.

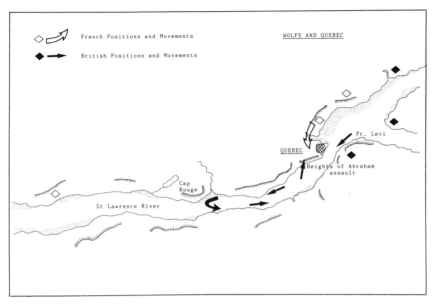

The bold battle strategy of General Wolfe in Quebec where, tragically, he met his death at the moment of victory.

the young officer's attentions were spurned by Miss Lawson in any case.

After taking part in another fight against the French at Rochefort, Wolfe was appointed a Brigadier and told to prepare for a voyage across the Atlantic. War had broken out between Britain and France in America in 1754, both countries laying claim to vast areas stretching from the east coast and the St Lawrence River to the Mississippi. Wolfe's task was to be a senior officer in a raid on the French fort of Louisburg near Cape Breton, a French enclave near what is now Nova Scotia. Commanding the expedition was Major-General Jeffrey Amherst, another Kent man.

In February 1758 they left England with 1,200 men and assembled at Halifax once they had crossed the Atlantic. There a large number of local people joined the Army, creating a poor impression on Wolfe: 'The Americans in the district are the most contemptible cowardly dogs. . . . They fall down dead in their own dirt and desert by battalions.' Wolfe led the landing at Cormorant Cove and after a very slow siege the French surrendered on 27th July. British dead numbered only 195. The whole expedition was a triumph.

On returning to England Wolfe found himself a hero, but also the victim of jealousy – though his high opinion of himself may not have helped. Army officers tried to tell the King that he was mad, but the King was not impressed by their views. 'Then I wish he would bite some of my other generals,' the King said, hoping that Wolfe's brand of madness would be passed on to his more lacklustre colleagues. Wolfe was, however, suffering from tuberculosis and kidney problems.

Wolfe's return to Britain also brought him a happier romance. He met Katherine Lowther at Bath and became engaged. Some said that he courted her because her uncle, Sir John Lowther, could confer political advantage.

By 1759 Wolfe was a Major-General and in charge of 9,000 men. He was to take part in an expedition planned to strike deep into French territory in Canada by sailing up the dangerous St Lawrence River to Quebec. He left England in February and once more sailed to Halifax.

Wolfe was well supported by the Navy, who got the whole fleet through the hazardous shoals along the river, and was able to anchor off the Isle of Orleans. A French attempt to beat him back using fireships after a hurricane had disrupted the fleet was a failure, and Wolfe captured good ground at Point Levi.

From Point Levi it was possible to bombard Quebec, but Wolfe's mission could have ended in disaster when the Grenadiers made an unplanned assault on the French, leaving Wolfe's position exposed. Then Wolfe himself was struck down by his kidney trouble, which may well have reached a terminal stage.

Wolfe was an impulsive soldier and found himself in a difficult position since expected support had not materialised. He had an emotional, even violent character and disliked being tied down. As long as the French stayed in their fortress, Wolfe was frustrated.

He cannot have been helped by the sight of his friend Jack Jervis performing heroics in the frigate *Porcupine*.

Perhaps the illness allowed Wolfe time to think, for a cunning scheme was certainly devised to take the French town. The plan was to land on the north bank above Quebec and capture the high ground of the Heights of Abraham, which commanded the approaches to the town. The slopes of the Heights were so steep that the French had left the position only lightly defended, but Wolfe knew there was a risk that any reinforcing of that defence could result in the massacre of his troops as they tried to scramble upwards. Secrecy was essential.

Who thought of this plan? It may not have been Wolfe but his brigadiers, Monckton, Murray and Townsend, who had become frustrated at the lack of progress.

The first thing was to confuse the French. Wolfe ordered his ships to move up and down the river to disguise his real movements. Under cover of all this to-ing and fro-ing, Wolfe took 3,000 men upriver to Cap Rouge. He must have known the dangers, for he left a treasured miniature of Katherine Lowther in the keeping of Jack Jervis. The French General Montcalm scoffed at ideas that Wolfe would try to scale the Heights: 'Only God can do the impossible, we cannot believe that they have wings that would allow them on one night to cross the water, land, climb rugged slopes and scale walls.'

At midnight on 12th September Wolfe started back down the river from Cap Rouge with 1,600 men, gliding along with the flow of the St Lawrence. Secrecy was such that he was nearly fired on by his own ships. The fleet set up a diversionary bombardment of Quebec. As Wolfe and his men slipped downstream in the darkness, he read the newly-published *Gray's Elegy*, being struck by the last line – 'The paths of glory lead but to the grave.' He confessed that he would rather be the poem's author than defeat the French.

His men crept ashore at Foulon Cove, anxious not to make a sound for the French were said to be guarding the Heights 200 feet

THE GREEN, WESTERHAM. 12383.

General James Wolfe's statue on The Green at Westerham, overlooking the place he knew so well in childhood.

above. But the French had left few men there and only one was awake, since they thought it impossible for an Army to scale the Heights. Within two hours Wolfe had 4,800 men on the Heights, extra troops having been rushed in.

From then on the French could be fought out in the open and Wolfe took part in the charge. He was hit in the chest after only ten yards and had to be carried to the rear. He was fading fast and knew it; 'Do not trouble,' he said, 'all is over with me.' Just as Wolfe lapsed into unconsciousness he heard a cry of, 'They run!'

All his lifetime's involvement with the Army caused him to revive at these words. 'Who run?' he asked, and was told that it was the French. 'God be praised, I die content,' Wolfe said, and soon passed away. The battle had lasted ten minutes.

His death at the moment of victory made him a national hero. Wolfe's body was brought home to Portsmouth and he was buried at St Alphege's church in Greenwich. A statue of him was erected at Westerham, overlooking the scene he knew so well in childhood.

EANSWITH
KENT'S FIRST
WOMAN SAINT

I N the early years of English Christianity, Kent managed to form quite a collection of saints. After both Augustine and Ethelbert had attained this status, there followed Kent's first female saint – Eanswith.

Eanswith was the daughter of Eadbald and grand-daughter of Ethelbert. Her father had led a wicked life, had lapsed back into paganism and was a notorious fornicator. He is reputed to have suffered recurring insanity and was plagued by an 'unclean spirit'. Eanswith was different altogether: from an early age she showed little interest in the prestige of being a princess. Whilst still a child she rejected 'worldly pomps and pleasures', showing marked preference for a life of cloistered peace and contemplation.

Eanswith decided to become a nun, but there were no convents or priories in Kent for her to join. However, she told her father, King Eadbald, about her vocation and he agreed to build a monastery close to the sea at Folkestone. According to legend, this became the first Benedictine priory in England.

Thus Eadbald's daughter turned her back on the world and on

the many marriage proposals she had received. She led a life of saintly peace; as Bishop Butler wrote, 'Her whole delight was in prayer and the love of God.' He also recorded that she spent her days in 'Holy retirement, perfect purity of mind and body, and the uninterrupted exercises of heavenly contemplation and prayer.'

Her father, Eadbald, who had begun his reign as an impious and sinful king, later repented. Two of Eanswith's brothers, Ermenred and Ercombert, shared her vocation and built their own monastery close to Eanswith's.

But of course a pious life was not enough to qualify a person for canonisation by the Roman Catholic Church. Miracles had to be performed. Eanswith is accredited with quite a number. One of her problems at the Folkestone priory was a shortage of fresh water; she apparently cured this deficiency by calling water to rise to the surface at a spot in a hillside a mile away, from which point it flowed in a stream down to where she stood. A number of wells and springs throughout this country and abroad have their origins explained by saintly miracles.

Another quite practical miracle of hers involved the building trade – not normally associated with saintly princesses. Some carpenters had been constructing a new building in Folkestone but had made the roof beam three feet too short – Eanswith arrived and miraculously lengthened it to just the right measurement. When a plague of ravens threatened to destroy the crops of Kent, Eanswith is said to have banished them rather as St Patrick banished snakes from Ireland. Eanswith's other miracles included restoring sight to the blind and casting out devils.

She died in AD 640 and was buried in the priory beside the sea. Three hundred years later it was wrecked by the Danes, but rebuilt in 1095. It was eventually destroyed again by the encroaching sea, but Eanswith's bones were moved to St Mary's church. Her annual festival is 12th September and her emblem is a fish, but she is also often portrayed beside her miraculous stream.

APHRA BEHN
INFAMOUS AUTHORESS

'A reproach to her womanhood and a disgrace even to the licentious age in which she lived.'

APHRA Behn became famous because of her plays, which were populated with highly lurid characters whose morals were distinctly questionable. Because of this it was believed that her own private life was just as dubious, but there seems a good deal of confusion as to just where fact and fantasy met in her life.

This extraordinary woman was born in 1640 at Harbledown, being baptised as 'Eaffry' Johnson. Both her Christian name and marital surnames seem to have gone through a variety of spellings during her life.

In 1663 she joined her mother in a voyage to the colony of Surinam. The experience was to form the background to her most celebrated novel, *Orinooko*, in which she described the tragedy of a black prince cut to pieces by savage Englishmen. Such was her reputation in later years that many people believed Aphra's story to be completely true, while others said that she herself had been the noble savage's mistress. No doubt such tales were good for sales.

Her stay in Surinam probably lasted only about six months, but it was long enough for her to form a close relationship with a colonist named William Scot. Scot's father had been involved in

Aphra Behn in her twenties, on the brink of achieving notoriety as a writer of lively and steamy literature!

the execution of Charles I and he had decided to avoid England for a while now that Charles II had been restored to his throne. It soon became 'popular knowledge' that he and Aphra were having an affair.

Aphra's time in Surinam was brief and she was soon back in England. She later said that on her return to England she married a merchant named Mr Behn, but others claimed that she invented him to give herself the respectability of a married name. He was certainly not around for long, but may have died in the Plague of 1665.

William Scot was, by this time, a 'wanted man', wisely staying abroad where he thought he was beyond the clutches of the Royalists. Aphra Behn was asked if she would take part in a scheme to entice secrets out of him, the bait being her own undoubted physical charms. It seems to have been assumed that Aphra's morals were such that she would have no qualms about using herself in this way.

She duly sailed from Gravesend on the *Castel Rodrigo* and went to Antwerp. She traced Scot but he was suspicious of her sudden arrival, nor was her position helped by a lack of finance. Scot refused to talk about his contacts unless a promise of a pardon was delivered to him, but the actual pardon never arrived and he was imprisoned for debt. Aphra's fate was no better – in fact exactly the same happened to her on her return to London!

Espionage was not to be her calling – literature was, though some critics called her work by less polite names. Having established a reputation for poetry, she then entered the lucrative field now called 'Restoration comedy'. This reflected the free and easy morality of Charles II's court, with much swapping of bedfellows amidst farcical events. The word 'bawdy' might have been invented just to describe these comedies.

Her first two plays were *The Forced Marriage* of 1670 and *The Amorous Prince* of 1671. Aphra showed she was equal to the demands of contemporary fashion – one of her plays started with two unmarried lovers getting out of bed while another even hinted at homosexuality.

In 1672 and 1674 she felt wealthy enough to visit the fashionable spa of Tunbridge Wells, and then fell in love with John Hoyle. Hoyle had been one of her social set in London, and was reported to have seduced Aphra before dropping her. Perhaps he was not an ideal partner in any case, for he has been described as 'an atheist, a sodomite professed, a corrupter of youth and a blasphemer of Christ.' It was generally presumed that Aphra shared the morals of her fictional characters and so was happy to mix with the likes of Hoyle, but she does seem to have been unfortunate with some of the men she encountered. Hoyle was stabbed to death in a pub brawl in 1692.

Her greatest success on the stage was *The Rover*, which was loved by James II. Her political plays, like *Sir Patient Fancy*, were not always as popular and some of her plays did not make it to the third night, when box-office takings went to the play's author.

In about 1682 she was commissioned by the Earl of Sheffield to write love poems to Princess Anne. Replies to these poems were written by Robert Gould, who suggested the matter could be resolved by Sheffield marrying Aphra Behn!

Her next venture was into the writing of novels, some of which were even more colourful than her plays. The first, about a society elopement scandal, was erotic enough to sell out 16 editions! *Orinooko* followed, and sealed her reputation as a writer of lively and steamy material.

Aphra Behn died in April 1689, some aspects of her life remaining an enigma to the last. Like Marlowe, her reputation has down the years led to her receiving less recognition in Kent than she might have deserved, but unlike Marlowe her name has not been rehabilitated.

'Sir William Courtenay'
Mad Messiah

ONE of the most tragic and bizarre characters in Kent's history is 'Sir William Courtenay'. Courtenay's real name was John Tom. He was born at St Columb Major in Cornwall in 1799, the son of a pub landlord. He was well-educated for someone of his class and his first job was as a solicitor's clerk. He married in 1821 and by 1827 was running a successful wine business in Truro. He was handsome, tall and strong, famous for his ability at cricket and wrestling – but there was a family weakness. In 1827 his mother went insane and died; soon afterwards, Tom himself began to suffer periodic bouts of insanity.

In 1832 he left Cornwall on a business trip to Liverpool and, after sending a letter to his wife, vanished completely. Mrs Tom placed advertisements in newspapers giving his description, but a year passed during which she heard nothing of him.

In fact Tom had assumed a new name and a new personality as the madness began to control him. Five months after disappearing in Liverpool, he turned up at Herne Bay off a steamer from London, then moved on to Canterbury. He had grown his hair long, developed a taste for exotic clothes and now called himself 'Count Moses Rostopchein Rothschild'. He booked in at the Rose

John Tom in the full princely regalia of his flamboyant alter ego, 'Sir William Percy Honeywood Courtenay'.

Inn but soon altered his name and titles, becoming 'Sir William Percy Honeywood Courtenay, Knight of Malta, Rightful Heir to the Earldom of Devon, and of the Kentish Estates of Sir Edward Hales, King of the Gypsies, and King of Jerusalem'!

In an attempt to establish his claims to the Hales estate, he visited the manor at Hackington but was ejected summarily. He made no attempt to lay claim to Malta or Jerusalem by personal visit, but wrote voluminously about his claims to the Devon earldom.

Courtenay became involved in politics more or less by chance, though he was an intelligent man aware of political life. The Tories in Kent were in a disorganised state since the Whigs seemed set to sweep the board in the Canterbury elections. In fact the Tories did not consider it even worth putting a candidate forward, except that the Whigs would then revile them for their weak surrender. The Tories therefore decided to approach the exotic stranger who had arrived in their city, not as a serious candidate but as a man who would deflate the self-satisfied Whigs by adding a touch of the ridiculous to the elections. Sir William graciously agreed to be nominated; no doubt he was pleased by the opportunities this would give him.

Courtenay showed an immediate skill as a master of the impressive-sounding but meaningless sloganeering of the time. References to 'England's Liberty', 'My character is my life' and 'I shall ever remain True Blue' peppered his speeches. He became wildly popular with the uneducated Canterbury crowds, who were impressed by his outlandish costume and eloquence. On one occasion they removed the horses from his coach and pulled it along themselves.

On the day of the election, Sir William appeared in a 'crimson velvet vest, richly trimmed with gold'. He still came bottom of the poll, with 375 votes compared to the two Whigs who got 834 and 802 each.

Courtenay was now bitten with an enthusiasm for politics and decided to stand in the East Kent election a few days later. By this time his ideas, some of which were wildly radical, had frightened the Tories. He had many ardent supporters among the lower classes, but the Reform Act had not extended the right to vote to such people. His campaign proved disastrous – out of about 9,500 votes cast, Sir William received only three.

Sir William was also short of money, having existed by using his charms to extort money from servants and maids at the inn. However, he found a temporary career as a celebrity, being paid to visit pubs and even taking part in a lecture tour of Kent that visited

Deal, Hythe and Folkestone. Then he teamed up with one Elijah Lazarus to produce a weekly paper called *The British Lion*; this characteristically mixed the ravings of a diseased mind with sound ideas – Courtenay advocated taxation according to means and the abolition of flogging in the British Army.

His defeat in the East Kent election had left Sir William in need of a new boost since his popularity seemed to be on the wane. In March 1833 he took part in a trial of smugglers at Rochester in which he first attempted to act as counsel for the defence and then appeared as a defence witness. After challenging a customs officer to a duel in Chatham, Courtenay was arrested for perjury and swindling. It was found that he had been at Boughton on the day he claimed to have been 'at sea', and one of the Canterbury servants who had lent him money had also laid a charge against him.

The arrest occurred in Canterbury and precipitated near-riotous scenes. A crowd gathered and threatened to riot unless their hero was released, forcing the Mayor to summon troops.

Courtenay was released a few days later and went to live at Fairbrook Farm, near Boughton, home of George Francis. He had to behave himself until he was due to appear for trial at Maidstone Assizes in July 1833. Francis was apparently 'a person of small understanding and little education, but of great pride and insatiable vanity.' His sister-in-law, who also lived at Fairbrook, developed a passionate attachment to Courtenay which seems to have been unrequited.

Courtenay's trial went badly. He angered the judge because of his tendency to talk endlessly, was found guilty and sentenced to seven years transportation. He also disappointed his supporters by grovelling to the judge when he realised his danger. However the trial brought publicity and one man made the connection between 'Courtenay' and the adverts for a missing Cornishman. The errant 'knight's' wife travelled up from Truro to Maidstone and was able to identify 'Courtenay' as John Tom.

In October 1833 he was transferred to the Kent County Asylum

The tragic scene at Bossenden Wood where the bizarre career of 'Sir William Courtenay' was finally ended.

at Barming, but Francis led a campaign for his release. William Tom, his father, agreed to look after him if released and on 3rd October 1837 he was discharged into his father's custody. However, 'Courtenay' did not like this arrangement, so it was agreed that he could go to Fairbrook instead.

This arrangement was no more successful. Tom soon reverted to his 'Courtenay' personality and incurred Francis' wrath by mixing with the labouring classes. When Francis threw him out in January 1838 – not taking kindly to Sir William's possession of two pistols – he soon found other friends to accommodate him. Bossenden Farm became a favourite haunt.

During the years of Courtenay's incarceration at Barming, the mood of the Kent labourers had worsened. Economic distress had caused them to take an active part in the Swing Riots of 1830–1, but the new Poor Law of 1834 threatened them with being confined to the workhouse if destitute, and the workhouse being built nearby at Herne was one of the most notorious in the country. Those who entered the workhouse lost their freedom and were separated from their families, making it a hated institution.

Courtenay soon understood the new current of desperation among the poor and set out to exploit it.

Early in 1838 he began to claim divine status for himself and some believed he was the new Messiah. Courtenay knew his Bible well, and could quote impressively from the Book of Revelations. He focused his attentions on the workhouses, prophesying that they and Canterbury would be destroyed by fire from Heaven. He cut his own hands, feet and side to reinforce the impression that he was the returned Christ.

On 27th May 1838 he collected a band of supporters together at Dunkirk, between Canterbury and Faversham – a remote, poor and backward part of the county which he knew well from his time at Fairbrook. He supplied these 'disciples' with beer and told them that in his care no bullet could hurt them.

Carrying a banner which depicted a loaf of bread stuck on a pole, with the clear inference that the poor demanded bread without being locked in the workhouse, a flag of blue and white, and a picture of a lion, the motley band began a march around the villages and farms of the district, demanding food and drink wherever they called. Courtenay interspersed the marching with philosophical pronouncements; one of these occurred when he took his shoes off and said, 'I now stand on my own bottom.'

On 29th May Courtenay led his followers on an aimless trek through the lanes to Selling before returning to his base at Bossenden Farm.

One of the 'disciples' was a servant who had left his work without permission, then a criminal offence. The Boughton constable, John Mears, had the duty on 31st May of going to arrest this man; due to the risk involved, Mears' brother Nicholas agreed to go with him. When they encountered Courtenay at Bossenden he shot Nicholas Mears and then attacked the constable with a knife. The latter escaped only because the deluded 'Messiah' tripped over. Then Courtenay returned his attention to the wounded Nicholas Mears, who he struck three times with his sword and then shot until he was dead.

Courtenay had crossed his Rubicon and his followers were horrified. He turned to them and shouted, 'I am the Saviour of the World. You are my true lambs – every one of you.' Pointing to the dead Mears, Courtenay continued, 'Though I have killed the body, I have saved the soul.'

In a few seconds a deluded madman had become a dangerous criminal threatening revolt and civil disorder. A hundred soldiers were summoned from Canterbury under the command of Major Armstrong, who was annoyed to find that a number of the local gentry had gathered to watch behind Bossenden Farm. One of the soldiers, Lieutenant Bennet, was sent to lead a flanking movement, but instead he attempted to talk to Courtenay. The 'Messiah' shot at him and missed, but a 'disciple' then shot Bennet and killed him.

George Catt from Faversham, a Special Constable, was the next victim, caught in the firing as he attempted to grapple with Courtenay. Armstrong warned the spectators away as a 'battle' developed.

Courtenay's followers were poorly prepared for a fight against the Army. The 'Messiah' had his pistols and one other man had a gun, but the rest were armed only with cudgels and farm implements. When Armstrong's men opened fire there was little they could do to defend themselves and within minutes the grass behind Bossenden Farm was littered with the dead and dying.

Sir William was killed with a bullet through the lungs and seven of his followers died in the battle, one more dying later. Of the forces of the establishment, Catt and Bennet were killed at Bossenden to add to Mears who died earlier. Altogether the career of Courtenay had brought twelve men to a sudden and terrible end.

The bodies of the dead 'disciples' were placed in the stables at the Red Lion inn nearby. A number were captured alive, including one who bled profusely from the mouth, moaning that Courtenay had promised bullets would not hurt them. Within hours sightseers began to arrive at the Red Lion and Sir William's bloodstained smock was torn into pieces as souvenirs.

That evening distraught women could be seen wandering through

Dunkirk and Boughton, bemoaning the loss of their men. Tragically, some expected them to rise from the dead at any moment as Sir William had prophesied could happen. But not even the 'prophet' himself showed any sign of a return to life, though a woman was arrested in an apparent attempt to revive him.

The event became national news and was debated in Parliament. Some feared that similar outbreaks of violence would be spurred on by the spread of the new Poor Law but attention gradually centred on why a lunatic had been released to cause so much bloodshed.

Significantly, those arrested were punished moderately for the times. Although the charges had included murder, none was executed. Instead, two were transported for life, one for ten years, and six received a year's hard labour.

The Courtenay affair sent a tremor of fear through the gentry and aristocracy of Kent, and indeed of England. Who was safe if bands of deluded labourers roamed the countryside under the leadership of madmen? Much was made of the poverty and ignorance of the Boughton district and in 1840 a new church was opened at Dunkirk. It was, in a way, Sir William Courtenay's memorial.

WILLIAM PITT
PRIME MINISTER

A large number of Prime Ministers have been associated with Kent, most famously Winston Churchill, who had a house at Chartwell near Westerham. More recently, Edward Heath was born at Broadstairs in 1916 and has held Kent constituencies throughout his political career. However, William Pitt was a Kent-born man who is unlikely ever to lose his claim to uniqueness as the youngest Prime Minister.

Pitt came from a political family. His father was William Pitt (1708–1778), later ennobled as the first Earl Chatham. Pitt the elder bought Hayes Place in West Kent as a country estate close enough to London not to interrupt his political career, and moved in shortly after his marriage to Lady Hester Grenville. The elder Pitt set about rebuilding the house and its grounds reflected his love of gardening. Apparently he quite often went out in the grounds at night to do some gardening if he had a sudden idea for an improvement. Such practices were not unusual among British Prime Ministers – Gladstone used to 'relax' by felling trees on his country estate.

On 28th May 1759 Lady Hester gave birth to her second son at Hayes Place, naming the child William. This was at the height of the elder Pitt's political career, during which he contributed to the success of the Seven Years War. Pitt later sold Hayes Place to Thomas Walpole, but bought it back again when he became ill since he was convinced that only the fresh air of Hayes would revive his health.

The young William Pitt also suffered from health problems and his parents decided he was too delicate to risk the rough-house atmosphere of a public school. Thus he learnt Greek, Latin and the skills of oratory from his father before going up to Pembroke Hall, Cambridge, at the age of 14.

The younger Pitt's health problems continued at university and a doctor recommended that he should take a quantity of port each day to alleviate his sufferings. The cure soon became worse than the cause, and Pitt's addiction to his 'medicine' caused him many problems in later life. Because of his health, Pitt graduated from Cambridge in 1776 without taking any exams. His father died in 1778, leaving him with the problem of how to live on an income of only £300 a year. Though Pitt went through all the procedures for taking up law as a career, he was devoted to entering politics, though this offered little prospect of sound financial return to one so young.

His attempts to become MP for Cambridge University in 1780 were frustrated, but four months later he secured election for the 'rotten borough' of Appleby. He took his seat at Westminster on 23rd January 1781, but he does not qualify as the youngest MP: Pitt's arch-rival, Fox, became an MP while only 19. Pitt was not lacking in ambition and in July 1782 was appointed Chancellor of the Exchequer in Lord Shelburne's ministry, having refused to consider any less prominent positions.

It was a time of considerable turmoil and confusion in British politics, not helped by King George III suffering from a sporadic illness that rendered him temporarily insane. George III hated one of the leading politicians of the day, Fox, so when Fox and Lord North succeeded in bringing down Shelburne's government the King turned to Pitt. The young Pitt turned down this offer to become Prime Minister because the balance of the Commons was

Walmer castle, where William Pitt lived as Lord Warden of the Cinque Ports from 1801 until his death in January 1806.

against him, and the task was taken up by Portland, though Fox and North were highly influential in his administration. Pitt, meanwhile, introduced a Bill for the reform of Parliament which he hoped would reduce the amount of bribery in British politics, though it also helped him to win some support away from Fox and North.

Another crisis occurred in the winter of 1783–4. A coalition led by Fox and North was defeated and Pitt was again invited to form a government. This time he agreed, but wanted Fox to join, though not North. Fox refused this arrangement and Pitt's first ministry began its life in a very weak position, unable to command a majority in the Commons. It sustained an early defeat in January 1784.

Pitt was Prime Minister at the age of 24, but was not short of political skill. The threat of abdication by George III was averted and Pitt gradually increased his strength in the Commons.

Later in 1784 new elections were held and Pitt became MP for Cambridge University. His position was much improved. With the support of the King and much increased strength in the Commons, he was in a strong position.

Pitt made various attempts to improve the collection of revenues and in 1784 introduced the East India Bill to supervise the East India Company's activities. He made a mistake, though, in instituting an enquiry into the conduct of Warren Hastings, who had governed Bengal. After seven years' legal entanglement, Hastings was cleared of injustice and oppression.

Pitt's foreign policy also had problems. His attempts to control the Russian grip on the Black Sea were outwitted by Catherine the Great, and his attempts to avoid war with France ended in failure when the French declared war in 1793. Fear that French revolutionary habits might spread to Britain led to the suspension of Habeas Corpus in 1794, making people liable to arrest without a fair hearing.

Pitt was a lonely and unlovable man in many ways and his private life reflected this. In 1796 he considered marrying Eleanor Eden but decided against it as he had debts of £300,000. A shortage of money was a permanent problem for him. By 1797 he was under great strain due to the pressures of the war against France and some of the press even alleged that he was going insane.

An outbreak of rebellion in Ireland in 1798 convinced Pitt that the administration of that province needed reform. He decided to unite the Parliaments of Dublin and London and used bribery to get the Dublin politicians to vote for the closure of their own House, its powers being transferred to Westminster under the Act of Union. However, George III refused to permit Catholics to take seats at Westminster, so on 3rd February 1801 Pitt resigned. George then went insane, later putting the blame for this on Pitt.

The same year Pitt's friends raised £12,000 to help him with his debts.

Pitt retired to Walmer Castle where he lived as Lord Warden of the Cinque Ports. During the invasion scare of 1802–3 he organised a local volunteer force.

In 1803 he was invited by Addington to join the government but refused to serve as anything other than Prime Minister. Thus he remained on the sidelines until he formed his second ministry in April 1804, again with uncertain support. His attempts to build a European coalition against Napoleon proved disastrous, collapsing in 1805 with the French victories at Ulm and Austerlitz. Though 1805 also included Nelson's victory at Trafalgar, the news of Austerlitz was a bitter blow from which Pitt never really recovered.

He died in January 1806, respected but never really loved. His later years had been troubled by illness, addiction to port and debts, while his coldness of character kept many social contacts at a distance.

After Pitt's death Parliament voted £40,000 to pay off the debts which had accumulated during his years of concentrating on politics.

SIR THOMAS WYATT
REBEL

T HE name of Wyatt achieved great fame in Tudor Kent. Sir Thomas Wyatt the elder, the son of a courtier, was rumoured to have been Anne Boleyn's lover in the 1520s. He died of pneumonia in 1542.

The younger Sir Thomas achieved even greater notoriety. He was born about 1521, and was related on his mother's side to the Lords of Cobham. He was brought up as a Catholic and in 1537 married the sister of the current Lord Cobham, Sir George Brooke. Ten children resulted from this marriage. But Sir Thomas was something of a wild character and marriage did not calm him. He had already demonstrated a 'wild and impulsive temperament', not helped when his father died and left him in charge of the estates at Allington Castle and Boxley Abbey.

His religious opinions may have been behind an incident in 1543, when Sir Thomas was arrested for breaking windows of London churches. He was also charged with eating meat during Lent, and spent a month incarcerated in the Tower as a result; he had clearly abandoned Catholicism by this time. The memory of these troubles was perhaps partially erased when Wyatt took part creditably in wars abroad, including the Siege of Boulogne in 1544.

The death of Edward VI in 1553 brought the Catholic Queen Mary, Catherine of Aragon's daughter, to the throne. When Mary

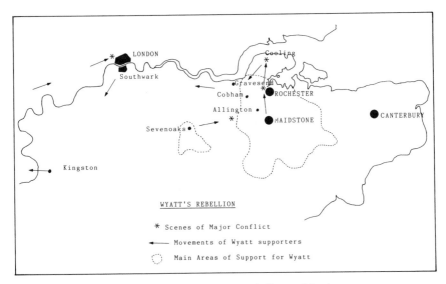

Map of the area where Sir Thomas Wyatt's rebellion took place.

announced her marriage to Philip of Spain it seemed likely that a new Catholic dynasty would be founded to rule England, in which the Spanish would play a key role. Wyatt decided he wanted none of this, and became involved in a plan to marry Edward Courtenay, the Earl of Devon, to the Protestant Princess Elizabeth and to overthrow Mary.

A number of Kent gentry shared Wyatt's views. They included Sir Harry Isley based at Sundridge and Maidstone, Robert Rudstone of Boughton Monchelsea, Sir George Harper of Chart Sutton and Henry Fane of Badsell. Wyatt met with some of these at Allington and on 25th January 1554 made an armed demonstration of protest at Maidstone. Mary's marriage had caused much dissatisfaction and Wyatt soon had 1,500 men, who he established in control of Rochester Castle. Some cannons were sent by boat from sympathisers in London, and these were placed so as to control the bridge across the Medway.

Not all went well however. Canterbury refused to join Wyatt's armed revolt and on 28th January men led by Isley and Knevett were defeated in a skirmish near Wrotham, with about 60 killed. They had been en route to join Wyatt at Rochester, but had been intercepted by loyalist forces which had gathered at Malling and which included the Mayor of Rochester, who had escaped from Wyatt's clutches.

When Queen Mary's advisers heard that Rochester was in rebel hands they determined on action. The Duke of Norfolk left London for Gravesend, intent on organising a counter-attack. At Gravesend he met Sir George Brooke, whose two sons had joined Wyatt. At this stage too, a deserter from Wyatt's forces joined Norfolk and told him about the rebels, saying, 'They are nothing. They are but a few and they know not what they will.'

A band of 500 Londoners under the command of Captain Bret were sent down to Kent to support Norfolk's efforts. Believing that Wyatt's men were of little value, Norfolk advanced to Strood on 29th January 1554. There, however, Wyatt's cannons deterred them from advancing too close to the bridge.

Wyatt's group at Rochester was clearly an army, not the band of confused rebels that had been suggested. Norfolk sent a herald forward to offer a pardon to any who surrendered, but he met with little response. So the Duke decided to attack, but the battle went disastrously for him. A large number of the Londoners went over to Wyatt and some of Norfolk's cannons were captured. He was forced to retreat to Gravesend. Meanwhile it was learnt that Wyatt had taken control of five Navy ships at Rochester.

Among those who went over to Wyatt's side was Captain Bret. Bret complained that this was all the fault of the Spanish. He said they would treat the English as 'slaves and villeins, despoil us of our goods and lands, ravish our wives before our faces . . .' and commit many other wicked deeds.

The next day Lord Cobham – Sir George Brooke – was aston-ished to hear the beat of a drum approaching Cooling Castle, and then to see Wyatt's standard leading his rebel army towards it. The large armed band stopped at the castle gate, and a demand that it should be opened was issued in 'the name of Sir Thomas Wyatt and all loyal Englishmen.'

Lord Cobham was not impressed. 'In the name of the Queen I do hold this castle,' he shouted back, 'and to none other will I render it.'

Wyatt spied out the land and discovered that the castle walls were weakest at the back, where it faced the Thames marshes. He took four cannons around there and began an assault, leaving two others at the front to bombard the gates. Poor Lord Cobham had only mustered a motley band of defenders, mostly servants and farmworkers, with only four or five handguns between them.

The cannons made short work of the castle defences. One ball smashed a hole in the gate, killing one man and wounding two others. Another shot through the chains holding the drawbridge up.

Cobham was later arrested by Queen Mary, who suspected that his defence of the castle had been rather unenthusiastic. His counter-claim was that in the heat of the battle he was betrayed by his own men, led by one 'Black Rob', who argued, 'Why should we fight for one master against another?'

In the six-hour siege five men were killed, then the rebels spent three hours plundering the castle. Cobham was taken captive and joined his sons with Wyatt's army.

The rebels marched towards London, reaching Dartford on 29th January and Deptford on 1st February. Cobham's sons then left Wyatt and succeeded in getting across London Bridge at midnight. They intended changing sides, but Mary's advisers considered them unreliable and put them in the Tower.

On 3rd February Mary declared Wyatt to be a traitor and £100 reward was offered for him. She offered to pardon all his supporters except Harper, Isley (or 'Iseley') and Rudstone (or 'Rudestone'). Wyatt replied by marching into Southwark, meeting no opposition from its people, and plundering the Bishop of Winchester's Palace.

The next day a 'banner of defiance' was unfurled at the Tower,

At Rochester Sir Thomas Wyatt captured several ships and took control of the castle. This enabled him to dominate the Medway bridge, though the castle's size is rather exaggerated in this early 19th century view. (Author's collection)

but its garrison was forbidden to fire across the Thames at Wyatt for fear of destroying innocent people's homes in Southwark. To show his contempt for Mary's reward, Wyatt had his name written on his cap so that prospective bounty-hunters could identify him.

On 6th February Wyatt left Southwark, apparently because its people were afraid of bombardment from the Tower. Wyatt marched to Kingston, hoping to cross the river, but 30 feet of the bridge had been broken down to stop him. However, after a short battle, he succeeded in getting boats across to the north bank.

Wyatt was running out of money and food – he needed success before his men began to desert him. His plan seems to have been to enter London or possibly capture St James' Palace, but deserters betrayed his plans. Harper, who had rejoined Wyatt, chose this moment to leave.

On 7th February there was a skirmish at the western edge of London with three of Wyatt's men being killed. The next day he marched along Fleet Street and up to Ludgate, but found the gates locked.

Wyatt went up to them and knocked, perhaps hoping that supporters in London would admit him. But only William Howard replied, saying 'Thou shalt not come in here.'

A quick battle then broke out, in which about 40 men were killed. The Queen had retained control of both London and the army, so with the situation looking hopeless Wyatt gave himself up. On 15th March 1554 he was sentenced to death and the execution took place at the Tower on 11th April. He was decapitated and quartered, but a few days later his head – put on display – was stolen. Bret was hanged in chains at Rochester.

JAMES JERSHOM JEZREEL 'PROPHET'

J AMES White was a soldier of obscure origins who enlisted in the 16th Foot Regiment and in 1875 was posted to Chatham as a preliminary to going to India. White must have been an unusual soldier for he showed no interest in the traditional military occupations of drinking and whoring, on which the prosperity of many Chatham residents was based. Instead White became interested in a sect called the 'New House of Israel' which had grown up to follow the teachings of the prophetess Joanna Southcott and later of John Wroe who had, however, been disgraced in 1830.

White visited some members of the sect called Head, who lived on Chatham Hill. He soon joined their group and began attending the meetings. Then on Christmas Eve 1875 he declared himself to be the 'Messenger of the Lord'. White announced that the next day he would read the first part of his prophetic message, which he called the 'Flying Roll'. This had apparently been composed during twelve days and nights of feverish activity in a house at Trafalgar Road, Gillingham.

The Heads were astonished by these claims and promptly expelled him. They were disconcerted when all 18 members of their sect then walked out and joined the new 'prophet'!

An artist's impression of Jezreel's Tower as it would have looked had it been completed.

White changed his name to James Jershom Jezreel and founded the 'New & Latter House of Israel', though they always tended to be called the 'Jezreelites'. He prophesied that 144,000 would be saved from death and that the end of the world was nigh. A time of trial and tribulation was expected, though he claimed that England would escape the worst troubles.

The formation of the new group was interrupted when Private 'Jezreel' was despatched to India in 1876, but he sent regular episodes from the 'Flying Roll' back to his disciples. None of his soldier colleagues were impressed by his transformation into a messenger of God.

Jezreel left the army in 1881 and returned to Chatham to marry

Clarissa Rogers, a girl born on Chatham Hill. He was over 40, she was 21 but had already ventured to America as an emissary for the sect. They set up home at 2, Copenhagen Road, Gillingham.

Clarissa soon convinced Jezreel to undertake a missionary tour of America using the help of a 'believer' named Noah Drew. Despite touring around in a waggon-train few converts were made; 'The pearl of truth was offered to many, but few received it,' Jezreel complained. On their return, the prophet and his wife toured Britain trying to poach members from Wroe's Christian–Israelite churches. They won over very few except in Lincoln, but an expedition to Australia was more successful.

After these travels, Jezreel decided to make Gillingham the world headquarters of his movement and opened a church at the corner of Nelson Road and Napier Road. Many members of the public came, largely out of curiosity – there was plenty of good music (led by Mrs Jezreel on the harp), children did most of the preaching, and the feet of the 'saints' were washed by the 'virgins'. Jezreel himself strode around carrying 'Peter's Keys' and a short iron rod, said to be a symbol of the Holy Spirit. Every 15 minutes a gong would be struck and a period of silence had to be observed.

Supporters abroad began to send money and Jezreel invested this in property in Woodlands Lane, Gillingham. In 1884 the 'Israel's International College' was opened there and open air meetings attracted crowds as large as 2,000 people. New converts were instructed to grow their hair long and keep it rolled up under a cap. The Jezreelites also started a network of shops including a bakery in Luton Road, a dairy farm, a smithy and a printer's.

One night Jezreel received a vision and was told to walk out into the streets. At dawn he came to a spot in the Darland district which seemed to be the highest point on the ridge overlooking Chatham and here Jezreel decided to build his headquarters. But he had reckoned without the military authorities, who refused to allow any 'tower' close to Fort Darland. So, instead Jezreel purchased some land nearer to the top of Chatham Hill from the Rock Freehold Land Society for £2,700.

Designs were prepared for a spectacular tower which had to be perfectly cubic, with all sides measuring 144 ft in every direction. Jezreel expected this building to be the place for the Second Coming. However, as built it only reached 120 ft high.

As the building rose up he arranged to have its walls decorated with symbols such as a trumpet, the Flying Roll and swords of the Spirit. It was planned to accommodate Jezreelite businesses like printing in the basement and then to have an assembly room for 5,000 as the main feature of the building. This would be covered by a glass dome and at its centre would be a circular platform which could be raised 30 feet upwards on hydraulics; this was for the choir and preachers. Total cost was expected to be £25,000 but money was flooding in from abroad and Jezreel was confident enough to start the building in 1885.

He had reckoned without divine intervention in the shape of a burst blood vessel, from which he died on 1st March 1885. His burial at the Grange Road cemetery was attended by 4,000 onlookers and the service was conducted by the Anglican curate. Mrs Head reappeared after his death to allege that Jezreel had been a bigamist, but no other wife could be found and attempts to blacken his name with scandal failed.

Would the Jezreelites fade away without their prophet or would a new one emerge? A brief power struggle took place with a Scot named Cummings as a contender for the position, but it was Mrs Jezreel who took over from her dead husband. She was now known as 'Esther Jezreel' but her liking for fine clothes and expensive carriages (which she occasionally attempted to drive with dangerous consequences) led to her being nicknamed 'Queen Esther'. Work on the tower continued, and the corner stone was laid in September 1885.

Money continued to arrive from Canada, Australia and New Zealand. By June 1887 the exterior of the tower was completed. Then the movement received another blow – in June 1888 Queen Esther died of peritonitis. Malicious rumours claimed she had died in childbirth but this was refuted by the doctor who attended her.

The *Chatham News* condemned the dead woman as a 'propagator of fanatical absurdity'.

The shadow of Jezreel did not depart from Gillingham with the death of the Queen. Two relations, Edward Rogers and Anne Rogers, struggled to control the movement – and its money. Edward Rogers won control of the Gillingham activities but fared badly. He failed to raise the money to complete the tower or even to hold on to the property and in 1905 the Jezreelites were evicted from their sacred place.

This time a new 'prophet' emerged in America. He was 'Prince Michael', who had joined the sect in 1888. He had claimed to be the new 'Messenger' in 1892 but had been rejected by Edward Rogers and had gone back to Detroit after a brief visit to Gillingham.

Prince Michael declared that he expected the 144,000 to be gathered at the Jezreel Tower at the end of time and managed to lease some of the old Jezreelite buildings in Canterbury Street. By 1909 his money had run out, however, and he was evicted. In 1912 he was fined 40s for assault but by 1914 had managed to get enough money to move back to the old base of Woodlands which Jezreel himself had used. However, in 1922 both Michael and his wife caught 'flu and died within days of each other.

Jezreel's Tower was left to crumble away until it was demolished in 1960. This was a great waste, for it was a unique and strange building with a fascinating history. It was also a fitting memorial to one of the strangest citizens ever to walk the streets of the town, and one of the most unusual men to feature in the history of Kent.

SAINT ELPHEGE
DEFYING THE DANES

ELPHEGE was a kind and peaceful man, devoid of earthly ambition, who rose to become Archbishop of Canterbury in years of great difficulty in the 11th century. He is held in high esteem in the history of Canterbury for his attempts to save the city from the murderous Danes.

Elphege was not born in Kent. He seems to have hailed from Gloucestershire, where he was born into a noble family and was thus able to enjoy a good education. While still a youth he decided to turn his back on worldly riches and enter a local monastery; the day he left his mother wept openly.

Elphege then decided that the monastery was too lively and distracting, so he built a remote cell for himself and lived as a hermit. But his godly ways were already attracting attention and his peace did not last. The monks of Bath Abbey were becoming notorious for their bad behaviour and Elphege was asked to become their Abbot.

When he took up the post he was appalled by the monks' behaviour and also found that they were reluctant to accept his discipline. However, the sudden death of one of the most difficult monks convinced the others that they were treading the perilous path that led to damnation, and they repented of their behaviour.

In AD 984 St Ethelwold, the Bishop of Winchester, died. Then St Dunstan, the Archbishop of Canterbury, had a vision in which he was approached by St Andrew and told that Elphege should be given the task of replacing Ethelwold. Elphege was appointed to the vacant see while still under 30 years old.

Elphege's association with Kent began in 1006, when he was appointed Archbishop of Canterbury. It was a time of great trouble and stress in England, with marauding Danes periodically terrorising whole areas of the country. It was one of these raids that led to Elphege's martyrdom.

A large army of Danes had been reported as marching towards Canterbury, intent on pillaging the city. Elphege was urged to leave, but he refused to desert the people of his city. When the Danes smashed their way into Canterbury and began slaughtering its people, Elphege demanded that they stop. They could kill him, he said, but not his people.

The heathen Danes were not impressed by this and chained Elphege up. They punished him by forcing him to watch the burning of the cathedral and the killing of the monks; then they beat and kicked him before flinging him into a dungeon.

The Danes stayed in Canterbury for several weeks, wrecking the city and terrorising its inhabitants. Then a plague broke out among the city's unwanted guests. Being a superstitious people, the Danes began to look for an explanation for this outbreak and they soon decided that Elphege was to blame; they dragged him out of his dungeon to see if he could explain himself.

Elphege blessed some bread and gave it to the sick Danes, who recovered miraculously. The Danes, however, were not very grateful – they offered to release the Archbishop, but only on payment of a ransom of 3,000 marks. Elphege refused to pay this on the grounds that the only gold he had was the wisdom of God's word. The Danes did not value this much as currency.

Elphege was taken to the main Danish base at Greenwich. There they knocked him down with the backs of their axes and began stoning him. Elphege, perhaps reminded of St Stephen,

Saint Elphege, who defied the Danes to defend the people of Canterbury in 1012.

tried to pray for them as they cast their stones at him. One of the Danes, though, had been moved by Elphege's courage and was more compassionate. Instead of allowing Elphege to die in the slow agony of stoning, he stepped in to finish off the Archbishop with an axe.

Thus died Elphege on 19th April 1012, and his body was interred at St Paul's. But his story does not end there. In 1023 his body was removed from its tomb and found to be 'entire' – miraculously it had not rotted in any way whatsoever. This was taken to be a sure sign that Elphege was a saint, so he was taken back to Canterbury and buried near the high altar.

WILLIAM ADAMS
SERVING THE SHOGUN

DESPITE its long connection with the sea and ships, Kent has numbered few explorers among its people over the centuries. One of the illustrious Kentish people who travelled to the other side of the earth was William Adams, whose story has been immortalised through the *Shogun* book and film.

Adams was born in Gillingham – the original part, down beside the Medway near the church and green. He was baptised in September 1564 but we know little else about him until he was apprenticed to Nicholas Diggins, a Limehouse shipbuilder, in 1576.

The apprenticeship was a long one, finishing only in 1588, but it taught Adams skills that undoubtedly saved his life years later. Having left the shipyard he became Master of the *Richard Duffield*, which acted as a transport ship during the Armada crisis of that year.

Adams' knowledge of the sea grew month by month as he sailed further afield, not even a wife – Mary – keeping him at home for long. In 1593–5 Adams took part in Dutch voyages to the North Cape of Europe, looking for a North East Passage to the eastern oceans. He also ventured on trading missions to the Barbary Coast.

In 1598 Adams joined another Dutch venture. Five ships were to set out for the Far East, and on 24th June Adams left on board the *Charity* with 110 men.

The little fleet was commanded by Jacques Mahu with Adams as pilot, changing from ship to ship. For a while he was on the *Hoop*, then moved to the *Liefde*. Perhaps this was just as well since the *Hoop* later vanished without a trace in the Southern seas.

Mahu died and was replaced by Simon de Cordes. The fleet sailed down the west coast of Africa and across the Atlantic, reaching the Magellan Straits in April 1599. There they wintered until September but the fleet was scattered by heavy storms and two of the ships returned to Europe.

Adams then proceeded northwards along the coast of Chile, which was ruled by the hostile Spanish. In a clash in November 1599 Adams' brother Thomas was killed and another of the ships was captured off Chile.

Clearly Chilean waters were dangerous and it was decided to cross the Pacific with the two remaining ships and seek a fortune in Japan. They set out into the world's greatest ocean on 27th November 1599, but the *Hoop* was lost during a storm on Christmas Eve.

Only 24 men survived the crossing to greet the coast of Japan when it appeared on the horizon on 19th April 1600. Only Adams and six others were strong enough to stand and gaze joyfully at the land.

They had arrived at a Japan that was still a feudal kingdom, though it had had contacts with Europe. The Emperors of Japan were having difficulty controlling their land as the rival clans fought for the right to call their leader 'Shogun'. The Shogun was the warlord in charge of defence and internal order – a powerful figure. However Portuguese Jesuits had established a foothold in Japan, and were anxious that Protestant heretics should be kept away.

When the *Charity* beached in Japan its crew of exhausted men were taken ashore and fed. The local lord sent word to Ieyasu, a powerful nobleman who coveted the title of Shogun. Through Ieyasu the Jesuits got to hear of the new arrivals and Adams claimed later that they tried to have him and the Dutch executed as pirates. However the priests did act as interpreters and since Adams could speak Portuguese he was sent to see Ieyasu. Although Japanese court etiquette was hard for a foreigner to understand Adams made quite a good impression, though he was still kept in prison for six weeks before being allowed to return to his companions.

What saved Adams from the plotting of the jealous Jesuits was his ability to build a ship. The ambitious Ieyasu thought that such a vessel would help his chances of becoming Shogun, and Adams built an 80 tonner for him. Ieyasu was delighted, and Adams was permitted to teach the warlord mathematics.

In 1603 Ieyasu became Shogun and Adams fared equally well. Ieyasu made him a noble, granted him an estate at Hemi-Miura and allowed him to marry a Japanese woman by whom he had two children. Of course his English wife was still alive. He also had another child by a mistress.

Adams' plans to leave in 1605 did not reach fruition, but he established contact with Dutch traders based in China. In 1609 Dutch ships visited Nagasaki and Hirado, and Adams helped in the negotiations which led to them being granted trading rights.

All was not easy however. The Jesuits, with their Spanish and Portuguese allies, hoped to oust the Dutch and bitter rivalry developed. Fortunately for Adams the captain of one Spanish ship, Vizcaino, created a bad impression on Ieyasu. Adams told the Shogun that the two greatest brigands on earth were the Pope and the King of Spain. In 1614 a Jesuit missionary tried to convert Adams by arguing about the unlimited power of prayer. To prove his point the Jesuit said he would use prayer to help him walk on water, but Adams had to rescue him from drowning. In 1614 Ieyasu banned missionaries.

Whilst these tussles were taking place, the British East India

Company was seeking a foothold in the Japanese market. In 1613 they set up a trading post at Hirado and Adams joined their payroll, though he did not get on well with the local captain, Saris.

Adams could have gone back to England at this stage, but balked at the final decision. Perhaps he realised that in Japan he was rich and powerful, whereas in England he would be a brief sensation and then forgotten. Saris did return to England, but was arrested for bringing pornographic books with him. Adams contented himself with trading voyages in the area.

In 1616 Ieyasu died and Adams found less favour with his son, Hidetada. The new Shogun disliked Adams, whose position was jeopardised when his wife was caught sheltering a Catholic priest.

Adams found restrictions being put on his trading activities, then he was assaulted by the Lord of Hirado. Some Japanese seamen also attacked him, saying they had been cheated by Saris. By 1618 Adams' influence was at an end.

William Adams died in 1620. In his will he arranged for some of his money to be sent back to his proper wife and daughter in England, but in many ways power and prestige had corrupted him when he had abandoned them for a new life on the other side of the world.

LOUIS NAPOLEON
EMPEROR OF FRANCE

CHARLES Louis Napoleon was born at the height of his uncle Napoleon Bonaparte's success, and eventually proved to be the only one of the family who lived up to the Bonapartist tradition in any way. He had a great number of connections with Kent and spent his last years in the county.

By the time the young Louis Napoleon had reached his teenage years, his family were classified as political undesirables in much of Europe. They were certainly not welcome in France, where the monarchy had been restored, and where attempts had been made to erase traces of the revolution.

As a political exile, Louis Napoleon spent some time in Italy and there became involved in politics for the first time. He joined an Italian nationalist group named the Carbonari and took part in the revolt in Rome in 1830. He was thrown out by the Papal Guard since the Papacy was sternly on the side of conservatism.

Like many political exiles down the years, ranging from the reactionary Prince Metternich to Karl Marx, Napoleon came to Britain because it was more tolerant than some other European nations. Though there was a new and more liberal monarchy in France after 1830, the name of Napoleon was still enough to incite opposition to a constitutional government and he remained persona non grata in his own country.

The exiled Prince Louis Napoleon with his wife, Eugenie, and son, the Prince Imperial, at Chislehurst in 1871.

On 10th May 1831 Napoleon arrived at Dover and then stayed in Canterbury. He moved on to visit London and Woburn, before returning to Kent in July. He and his mother went to Tunbridge Wells and stayed at the Royal Kentish Hotel before renting a house. Always a womaniser, Napoleon employed his Gallic charms on a visiting English girl.

In August he departed for Switzerland but by November was back in London and beginning a round of political plotting. This culminated in October 1836 in his involvement in a revolt at

Strasbourg, in eastern France. He was arrested and packed off to the USA.

America was too far from France, so Napoleon came straight back to London in July 1837. After another visit to Switzerland he settled down in the British Museum to work on his book, *Des Idées Napoliennes*, which was to be the basis for his appeal to the French lower classes.

During this stay in England he met Benjamin Disraeli, the MP for Maidstone. Disraeli wrote about him as 'Prince Florestan' in his novel *Endymion*. Also during this time he began to make his first visits to Chislehurst to see a lady named Emily Rowles. The small Kent town was eventually to become his home.

On 3rd March 1840 Napoleon had to fight a duel with pistols on Wimbledon Common, but was arrested before a shot could be fired. Prince Napoleon was bound over in the sum of £500.

This was not furthering his ambitions, so he decided on more positive action. Feeling that it might need only a spark to ignite France in his favour, he decided to stage another revolt. He chartered the steamer *Edinburgh Castle* and set out from Gravesend. After calling in at Ramsgate, he sailed to Boulogne where he intended to strike his first blow for Bonapartism.

It was another disaster. He was captured and imprisoned at Ham. Emily Rowles sent parcels to him there and he was allowed access to a mistress, so life cannot have been too harsh. Indeed it was lax enough for him to escape in May 1845 and he soon returned to England. There he fell in love with a courtesan named Elizabeth Howard, who later followed him to France and was made Comtesse de Beauregard in 1853.

In 1848 France was plunged into political turmoil once again and Louis Napoleon made sure he was on the scene. The collapse of Louis Philippe's monarchy was followed by much bloodshed in Paris, and then elections for the Presidency were held. Louis Napoleon trounced all opposition. Within a few years he had overthrown the constitution he was meant to rule and had declared himself Emperor Napoleon III.

What sort of man was he? Certainly not impressive to look at. One English guest saw him as 'a short, thickish, vulgar-looking man without the slightest resemblance to his imperial uncle or any intelligence in his countenance'. Yet he certainly must have had some form of charisma as his remarkable series of romantic conquests testifies. When Queen Victoria met him in 1852 she wrote that, 'With such a man one can never for a moment feel safe.' In 1855, after a drive through the Bois de Boulogne with him, she recorded, 'I felt – I do not know how to express it – safe with him.'

Napoleon III's rule over France was long – long enough to suggest that he was more intelligent than some critics thought. He rebuilt much of Paris through the work of Baron Haussmann, though much of the energy of the time was frittered away on immoral activities as described in Zola's *Nana*. In March 1855 Napoleon visited England, dining in Dover at the Lord Warden Hotel where the celebrated novelist W.M. Thackeray peered at him. On the way to London he got off the train for a few minutes at Tonbridge and waved to workmen.

After 1860 he was increasingly troubled by illness and in the last years of the decade was unable to resist pressure to declare war on Prussia. The war, which started in 1870, was largely provoked by Bismarck through his notorious 'Ems Telegram', worded to insult the French. Bismarck, and probably Napoleon as well, knew of French weaknesses but demands for war were led by the Empress Eugenie herself. Napoleon was too ill to resist and the war was a disaster.

Joining his Army at the front, Napoleon was unable to prevent his troops becoming encircled at Metz and then he himself was captured by the Prussians at Sedan. The Empire collapsed around him and his family fled to England.

The ex-Emperor was held by the Prussians, but his family were more fortunate. On 6th September 1870 his son, the Prince Imperial, arrived at Dover and then went by train to Hastings. There he was joined by Eugenie, the deposed Empress. The task of finding them a home was left to a Dr Evans. At first he considered Tunbridge Wells as Napoleon had liked it, but then he found Camden Place in Chislehurst – now part of the Golf Club.

Camden Place had an interesting history. A previous owner had been a Russian merchant named Bonar, but in 1813 he and his wife had been murdered by a footman. The owner in 1870 was Strode, who had been a trustee for the courtesan Miss Howard.

On 20th September Evans and the Prince Imperial visited Camden Place and approved of it. They arranged to take it, and soon Chislehurst attracted a small French community.

On 30th November Queen Victoria and Princess Beatrice came to inspect it too. The Queen described it, 'Everything was like a French house and many pretty things about.' Victoria was also struck by the change in Eugenie:

'She looks very thin and pale, but still very handsome. There is an expression of deep sadness in her face, and she frequently had tears in her eyes.'

A French-speaking priest was appointed to the Chislehurst Catholic church.

On 20th March 1871 the Chislehurst stationmaster, Mr Lord, arrived at Camden Place with the news that Napoleon would soon be arriving in England. A special train was arranged to take Eugenie to meet him at Dover. A curious coincidence occurred at Dover where the Napoleon family, fleeing from France, met members of the Orleans family who were returning there now that Napoleon was defeated.

Thus on 20th March 1871 Napoleon returned to Kent and on 3rd April Queen Victoria came by train to Camden Place. Though she was pleased to see the family she found that the rooms were overheated. Discreet hints were made to Napoleon's staff about future visits depending on room temperature.

Napoleon was still popular with women and an eccentric

Camden Place, Chislehurst, where the Imperial Family made their home. Queen Victoria visited them there, remarking later that 'Everything was like a French house and many pretty things about'.

widow came each day to lay flowers at the gate. Napoleon had the chance to learn about cricket as the West Kent field was close to his home.

In April 1872 Queen Victoria made another visit, but then Napoleon's health faded and he rarely left the house again. Even so it was rumoured that French spies kept track of all activities from the nearby windmill.

On 2nd January 1873 he had an operation at Camden Place to remove a bladder stone, and another operation on 6th January. They were unsuccessful, and Napoleon died on 9th January 1873. His funeral was held on 15th January and he was buried in a special mausoleum at Chislehurst.

The Prince Imperial died in the Zulu wars in South Africa but Eugenie lived on into another era altogether, only passing away in 1920.

RICHARD DADD
ARTIST IN TORMENT

ICHARD Dadd's story is as strange as that of any artist. Once reckoned to be on the threshold of a brilliant career, he suffered such mental troubles that he was said to be 'classed among the dead'. However, in more than 40 years in various institutions he continued to paint and over a century after his death is finally being accorded the status his talent deserves.

Dadd was born in Chatham on 1st August 1817, the son of an apothecary. He was one of seven children, of whom four were to die insane. Clearly, therefore, his own later troubles were not the result of supposed 'exposure to the sun' but due to genetic inheritance.

Dadd's father Robert was a cultured man who was active in the local Literary and Philosophical Institution, starting a museum in 1827. He could afford to send Richard to the King's School in Rochester, where he became interested in the Classics.

Richard Dadd started to draw at about the age of 13, and the Medway landscape formed a background to his pictures even in his later years. Rochester Castle, Medway shipping and the local countryside all captured his imagination; a favourite spot for sketching expeditions was the Darnley estate at Cobham.

In 1834 the Dadd family moved to London where Robert Dadd

began a new business. They lived in a quite prosperous street off Haymarket and young Dadd was able to meet many other artists. In December 1837 he became a student at the Royal Academy. While at the RA he became a close friend of Frith, who was most impressed with Dadd's character and ability:

'Dadd was my superior in all respects; he drew infinitely better than I did . . . I can truly say, from a thorough knowledge of Dadd's character, that a nobler being, and one more free from the common failings of humanity, never breathed.'

One of Dadd's sisters married another artist colleague of his, John Phillip. She too went mad and tried to strangle her child. From 1863 until 1893 she was kept in an asylum at Aberdeen.

Dadd and his friends formed their own group called 'The Clique', but most considered Dadd to be their leader in talent. By 1840 he was exhibiting his work regularly and already showed a fascination with fantasy with works based upon *A Midsummer Night's Dream*. Another inspiration for him was Byron's poem *Manfred*, with its visions of demons and madness.

In 1842 Dadd went on a voyage to the Middle East with Sir Thomas Phillips, a Welsh solicitor who had gained fame during a Chartist revolt. Dadd was expected to record what they saw in sketches, providing himself with some basic material which he continued to use for the rest of his life. Rocky passes and ruined castles continually appear in his work as memories of his journeys.

After Greece, Turkey and Rhodes they travelled into Lebanon in extreme weather conditions. At Jericho they were nearly imprisoned by Arabs before making a more relaxed journey along the Nile.

Later people claimed that exposure to the Egyptian sun caused Dadd's illness, and he does seem to have encountered his first problems while in that country. Before he reached Egypt he had written to Frith about his mind being 'so full of wild vagaries that . . . I truly doubted my own sanity.' In Egypt his mind seems to have passed over the brink, and for the rest of his life Dadd's madness seems to have been haunted peculiarly by Egyptian visions.

On the return journey he became depressed and was convinced that he was being pursued by spirits which disguised themselves as old ladies or priests. By May 1843 he seems to have virtually lost control of himself.

His friends and family found Dadd changed totally on his return. He had become gloomy, unpredictable and sometimes violent, once cutting a mark from his head that he said the Devil had placed there. He told a friend that he was haunted by evil spirits, notably the Egyptian god Osiris.

From June to August 1843 his behaviour worsened. He lived almost entirely on beer and eggs, simply throwing the shells on the floor of his rooms. He drew a number of pictures of his friends, all with their throats cut. His father hoped that Richard's illness would pass and therefore agreed to go down to Kent on 28th August.

Richard Dadd definitely decided to kill his father before making the trip, since he bought an eight-inch knife and a cut-throat razor in advance. They booked rooms at an inn in Cobham, later a haunt of Dickens, and then went for a peaceful evening stroll in Cobham Park where the young Dadd had enjoyed sketching.

The next morning Robert Dadd's body was found by a Rochester butcher, who had at first thought him to be a drunk sleeping off the previous night's excess. Both knife and razor were found nearby.

Richard Dadd had not returned to the inn but had gone straight to Rochester, where he booked in at the Crown Inn to wash the blood off himself. After a brief return to London he left England by hiring a boat at Dover for £10. Almost as soon as he had fled, one of his brothers, George, had to be sent to Kensington House Asylum showing similar behaviour to Richard.

Dadd was too ill to escape the authorities for long, especially as he was often under the impression that other people were the Devil in disguise. This was why he had attacked his father, and it may also explain his attack on another passenger in a coach near Fontainebleu in France. This time Dadd was captured and whilst in custody spent many hours staring at the sun or conversing with an imaginary person.

He was brought back to England in March 1844, making court appearances at Rochester and Maidstone. These were formalities, for all knew he was insane and some expected him to die at any time. In August 1844 he was admitted to the Bethlem Hospital, expected to disappear into the world of the 'dead'.

Within a year of being admitted, Dadd began to paint again and from 1853 was encouraged in his work by Dr William Hood. George Haydon also showed interest in him and Dadd dedicated two of his greatest paintings to these two men.

In 1864 Dadd was moved to the newly-opened Broadmoor but this made little difference to his work, which depended almost entirely on his imagination. He spent the rest of his time there playing the violin and reading.

Dadd never really recovered from his illness. Throughout the time at Broadmoor he continued to show an uncontrollable temper and was occasionally violent. Though he spoke of it less often, he still believed himself to be pursued by Osiris.

In late 1885 Dadd became ill with consumption and he died in January 1886. His sister Mary Ann wrote from America to say that she was thankful that he was at rest and no longer in the insane condition which for her had meant 'his life has been to me a living death.'

After Hood died in 1870 some of Dadd's paintings which he had collected were sold, fetching a maximum of 36 guineas. Relatively little interest was aroused by them, though Dickens had known all about Dadd and liked to take his guests to the scene of the murder in Cobham to re-enact the event. Dadd's real fame had to wait until the 20th century, and interest in his work has increased considerably. In 1974 a special exhibition about him was held at the Tate Gallery.

SIR PHILIP SIDNEY
THE PERFECT KNIGHT

S IR Philip Sidney rose to fame as a favourite of Queen Elizabeth and was a typical adventurer of his day. Spenser,
the Elizabethan poet, referred to him as 'the president of
nobless and chivalry'. Sidney added a touch of refinement to a
Kent aristocracy battered by the troubles of the Tudor years.

Sidney was born at Penshurst on 30th November 1554 and
was able to claim Philip of Spain, Queen Mary's husband, as his
godfather. No doubt this was something the family kept quiet
after the Protestant Elizabeth had succeeded Mary on the throne
of England.

Sidney was a member of a family which took full advantage of
the customary aristocratic privileges of the day. He spent a de-
lightful childhood at Penshurst, which was not interrupted by his
being appointed Rector of Whitford in Flintshire when he was
just over nine years old. The benefice was secured for him by
his father, the result being that young Philip could claim £60
per year while some poor curate took the actual services for a
pittance.

In 1564 Sidney was sent to Shrewsbury school and in 1568 to
Oxford. He divided the rest of his time between the family homes
at Ludlow and Penshurst. He also benefitted from the attention

of Sir William Cecil, who was close to the Queen and took a personal interest in the charming young man from Kent.

To complete his education, young Sidney went abroad. He had the misfortune to be in Paris in 1572 during the St Bartholomew's Day massacre, when many French Protestants were murdered. He continued his travels to Austria and Hungary, returning home a convinced Protestant. What his godfather thought of this is not recorded!

Back in England, he took up a life as a courtier, though in 1576 Elizabeth sent him on another European mission to see Emperor Rudolph. Sidney was troubled by a lack of personal income and was sufficiently embarrassed to have to send his bills to his father for payment – even something as modest as a pair of boots was beyond his means.

Such a cultured and chivalrous young man inevitably became involved in a love affair. His passion was for Penelope, daughter of the Earl of Essex, to whom he sent many sonnets – the true Elizabethan lover. However, she married someone else, so perhaps she did not have a poetic temperament.

In 1578 Sidney put his imaginative genius into a fantastic 'masque' held at Wanstead House, east of London. Elizabeth was portrayed in it as 'The Lady of May' and Sidney ensured his place as a favourite.

In 1579 he was busy enlarging Penshurst for his father, but then hit a period of trouble. He became embroiled in a row with the Earl of Oxford and also criticised the suggested marriage between Elizabeth and the Duke of Anjou. Elizabeth was notorious for her temper – just like her father – and Sidney was banned from her presence. Deprived of the court life which he so loved, he devoted his time to poetry. The result was *Arcadia*, a romance in prose and verse.

On 16th January 1581 Sidney was elected MP for Kent, but as MPs were unpaid this did not help his perennial cash crisis. He was able to get back into Elizabeth's favour however and in 1581 took part in jousts to celebrate a visit by the Duke of Anjou.

1583 was a momentous year for him. Sidney was knighted by Elizabeth and in September he married a girl of 14 who was the daughter of Lord Walsingham – Sir Philip was twice her age.

Stories had been reaching England about the wonders of the Americas, and Sidney became fascinated by them. He supported a number of voyages and once had 3,000,000 acres 'assigned' to him. In 1585 he laid plans for a trip to America with Drake, presumably to inspect his 'estates' there, but Elizabeth summoned him back before he had got any further than Plymouth.

On another occasion there seemed a chance that Sidney would be elected King of Poland, and this also displeased Elizabeth. According to the historian Camden, she feared 'that she would lose the jewel of her times'.

On 7th November 1585 Elizabeth appointed him Governor of Flushing, now known as Vlissingen; this was in a part of the Netherlands then embroiled in a conflict with the Spanish. Elizabeth also promoted him to General of the Cavalry and on 16th November 1585 Sidney left from Gravesend to take up his new post.

He soon showed a lively interest in military affairs, taking part in a night attack on the Spanish garrison in the town of Axel.

On 22nd September 1586 Sidney took part in the Battle of Zutphen. His friend Pelham had come without any leg armour so Sidney, always chivalrous, insisted on lending his own. In the battle Sidney's horse was shot from under him and so he mounted another but then he was wounded in the thigh himself.

As he lay in agony, Sidney asked for water but then saw a dying man gasping. 'This man's need is greater than mine,' Sidney said, and refused the proferred drink.

The thigh wound became gangrenous and Sidney lapsed into serious illness. As he lay on his deathbed he composed a short poem, which was set to music and performed to him as he lay dying. The end came on 17th October 1586.

Even after his death the old money troubles haunted him, delaying his funeral for three months. Eventually Sir Philip Sidney, courtier and poet, was laid to rest in St Paul's cathedral.

ELIZABETH BARTON
THE NUN OF KENT

THE story of Elizabeth Barton is one of the most extraordinary in the history of Kent. From a very humble background, she had the opportunity to talk with the highest and mightiest in the land before suffering an awful death. It is also perhaps surprising that she was never canonised a saint.

Elizabeth Barton was probably born at Aldington in 1504 and by the early 1520s was employed on the Goldwell estate by Thomas Cobb, probably as a servant. Cobb farmed land for the Archbishop of Canterbury.

In the spring of 1525 Elizabeth became very ill, her throat swelling strangely and causing her to writhe in agony. Then she developed fits which lasted for seven months despite all the efforts of the local priest, Richard Master, a Maidstone man. In November 1525 she started talking from her sickbed, and prophesied the death of a young child in the district. The event occurred almost immediately after she had foretold it.

This attracted great attention to Elizabeth, but her illness continued. She would lie in deathly stillness, then suddenly throw herself around in fits. A voice was heard 'speaking within her belly', creating a mystical effect: 'it spake so sweetly and heavenly that every man was ravished with the hearing thereof.'

Elizabeth Barton was questioned at Archbishop Warham's Palace at Otford. These foliage-covered ruins were all that was left of the Palace when this sketch was done in 1885. (Author's collection)

The voice intoned words about Heaven and Hell, sin, attendance at church and the Virgin Mary.

These pronouncements attracted yet more attention and Master informed the Archbishop of the events. Opinion, though, was divided; were her words from God or the Devil?

Elizabeth then began to make pronouncements about the little chapel of Court-at-Street, south of Canterbury on the old Roman road. A hermit tended it, and Elizabeth revealed a miraculous knowledge of his eating habits. When she prophesied that her illness could be cured by taking her there she was despatched with all speed, but no cure occurred.

The Archbishop sent some learned monks to study her case and they found her to be a good Catholic. In early spring 1526 Elizabeth was taken to the chapel again and, in front of a statue of Mary, she was healed miraculously. This time her fame spread to London, reaching the ears of Henry VIII and Sir Thomas More.

An Aldington farmhouse was clearly no place for such a phenomenon and Elizabeth was taken to St Sepulchre's Priory in Canterbury. There she continued to have visions and trances, often making 'trance visits' to the little chapel of Court-at-Street. A 1527 book called *A Marvellous Work* even cast her and the Virgin Mary together in the joint leading roles.

However, Protestantism was beginning to stir among the English and not everyone was impressed with her. In 1528 William Tyndale, the Biblical scholar, declared her prophecies to be the Devil's attempts to deceive the faithful. This did nothing to deter pilgrims who flocked to the little chapel, from which further miracles were reported.

In September 1528 the 'holy maid' declared a wish to talk to Cardinal Wolsey. Early in October she travelled to London and told Wolsey that it was his duty to preserve Henry's marriage to Catherine of Aragon, the marriage by then being under pressure due to Henry's lack of a male heir. Whether she met Henry himself at this time is debatable, but she is alleged to have declared that 'the vengeance of God would plague' Henry if he married Anne Boleyn. When she returned to Canterbury, Elizabeth predicted the downfall of Wolsey and this duly occurred – though it was already looking likely when she visited London.

Between December 1529 and January 1530 she was again in London and certainly met Henry, who was fascinated with religious issues. She told him that if he married again he 'should not be King long of this realm'. On the way back to Canterbury, the 'holy maid' visited Bishop Fisher of Rochester, on whom she made a good impression.

Already, though, the religious state of the nation was becoming a political issue. In 1531 Henry began his attack on the Catholic clergy, including Fisher. In fact an attempt was made to poison Fisher, two people dying though the Bishop escaped. His cook was arrested and 'poached' in a cauldron of boiling water, but persistent rumours blamed the Boleyn family.

Elizabeth Barton had powerful protectors in Canterbury, including two senior ecclesiastics named Goldwell and Bocking. he had now developed a reputation for uncovering other people's sins – she once intervened to stop three monks from committing adultery. Wolsey had died, but Elizabeth claimed to have saved his soul by 'mediation'. Uncharitable critics suspected the motives of Goldwell and Bocking however, some suggesting that the latter was her lover.

In 1532 she had a vision of Archbishop Warham dying and going to heaven, and he helpfully died on 23rd August. When Henry VIII passed through Canterbury in September she was said to have told him that he would 'die a villain's death'. Anne Boleyn was told that 'Dogs will eat Jezebel in the town ditch of Jezreel.' Then Elizabeth claimed to have been 'transported' to Calais to take part in the eucharist with Henry himself.

As the crisis of Henry's matrimonial affairs developed, Elizabeth became more provocative in her prophecies. She declared that the crowning of Anne Boleyn as Queen would begin the last month of Henry's reign. Fisher, though, formed the opinion that she had allowed Henry seven months' grace.

Anne Boleyn was crowned on 1st June 1533 but Henry was still King on 1st July. However, on 4th July the Pope excommunicated Henry unless he repudiated the marriage to Anne, so Elizabeth could say that Henry was no longer King in the sight of God.

Henry was becoming concerned about the 'holy maid' and her prophecies and ordered Thomas Cranmer, his new Archbishop, to investigate. Cranmer summoned Elizabeth to Otford where he was staying.

In the autumn of 1533 Elizabeth Barton and various priests who had supported her were arrested. She had made the mistake of becoming involved in politics as well as religion, partly due to the involvement of Lady Exeter. Among the others arrested were Father Bocking of Canterbury and Master, the Rector of Aldington.

Paul's Cross in London: Elizabeth Barton and her Catholic accomplices were denounced here on 23rd November 1533.

The 'holy maid' was questioned in the Tower and at Lambeth Palace by Thomas Cromwell, Archbishop Cranmer and Bishop Latimer. They were astonished when she declared openly that all her visions were false! However, she was later to state that an angel had appeared and instructed her to deny the truth of all her visions – the reason for this is unclear.

In November 1533 she was examined by the Privy Council and confessed to treason and heresy. She even showed them how she distorted her face to simulate the ecstatic fits which preceded her prophecies.

On 23rd November wooden staging was put up at Paul's Cross in London. Elizabeth, Bocking and other offenders were led out in chains and a sermon preached denouncing them. Many details were given about how the 'holy maid' had used chemicals to make smells and smoke which were meant to be evidence of devilish visitations. All of the accused were then made to read out written confessions.

On 7th December Elizabeth Barton did penance in Canterbury and in March 1534 was condemned to death. Others sentenced included Master, Bocking and four others – all for treason. It was said that they had used Elizabeth's prophecies to encourage rebellion against the King and his new Queen.

On 20th April they were all taken to Tyburn where the maid was hanged until dead (the others being cut down while still alive) before being beheaded. The other clergymen who had supported her were executed in a terrible and brutal fashion.

So ended Elizabeth Barton's extraordinary career – it is certainly one of the strangest stories ever associated with a Kent woman.

WAT TYLER
& THE PEASANTS' REVOLT

THE Peasants' Revolt, which was largely a protest against taxation, is usually said to have started in Essex during the late spring of 1381. The 1370s had seen England involved in expensive wars which had to be paid for somehow. Richard II became King in 1377, but could hardly be blamed for the situation since he was only ten years old. However, his advisors introduced the hated Poll Tax, levying a rate in 1377 and 1379 on all adults. In 1381 they increased their demands three-fold, asking for one shilling a head from rich and poor alike.

The Poll Tax was simply the latest in a long line of troubles that the peasantry had had to face, at a time when the Black Death had decimated the population. The revolt soon spread across the Thames to Erith, where a retired soldier named Abel Ker sympathised with its aims. Ker got a band of rebels together and raided the local monastery, where they frightened the abbot into swearing support. A boat was sent across the Thames to Barking to recruit more supporters, then Dartford was raided.

A Dartford baker named Robert Cave took over the leadership from Ker. Cave made a bold decision to march to Rochester and storm the castle, but his men made little impression. However, its Constable, Sir John Newton, foolishly agreed to let the rebels inside for 'discussions' – once inside they plundered the place and freed its prisoners from the dungeons.

One of those released was John Belling. Belling had been a serf – virtually a slave under the old feudal system – who had run away from Gravesend but then been recaptured. The hatred of serfdom was another major impetus behind the revolt, for the Black Death had severely reduced the nation's labour supply and the lower orders had become more aware of their value.

The rebels then moved on to Maidstone, where they executed William Topcliffe and John Southall, two leading citizens. At this stage Cave fades out of the story, though he had played a large enough part to later get 10 years in prison. He was replaced by Wat Tyler.

It is generally agreed that Tyler became a rebel because of events involving his daughter. The girl was only 14, but the collector of the Poll Tax claimed that she was older and so would have to pay. He then rudely tried to demonstrate that she was older than Tyler claimed by pulling up her skirt – which Tyler tried to stop. The tax collector struck at him with a stick and Tyler, probably an ex-soldier, killed him.

By 8th June the rebels were in control of much of Kent. They took the chance to pay off some old scores, punishing anyone thought to be a supporter of the hated John of Gaunt. Official documents were stolen in Strood and Dartford, to be burnt in the street. A manor at North Cray was burnt down and some gentry taken hostage.

On 10th June Tyler led a march on Canterbury. The Palace of the Archbishop, Simon Sudbury, was pillaged and a priest named John Ball released from the Archbishop's prison. He became the rebels' chaplain and was author of a famous couplet about the origins of the class system:

> 'When Adam delved and Eve span,
> Who was then the Gentleman?'

The Sheriff of Canterbury was assaulted and soon revolts were breaking out elsewhere in the county – at Tenterden, Appledore and Sandwich. Many supporters joined the rebels in Canterbury, one of the more famous being Jack Straw.

The rebels left Canterbury and returned to Maidstone, which they ransacked thoroughly. Then they marched towards London. On the way they came across the Countess of Kent, the King's mother, but according to tradition, all they demanded of her was a kiss. On 12th June the rebels camped at Blackheath, from where they sallied forth to loot Lambeth Palace.

King Richard, being only 14, was hardly prepared for such a challenge – though his age probably saved him from being blamed for the peasants' troubles. He was taking cover in the Tower when Walworth, the Lord Mayor of London, suggested sending three men to Blackheath to talk to the rebels. However, some of the rebels wanted revenge rather than discussion; John Ball, for instance, was anxious to revenge himself on the Archbishop, Simon Sudbury, who was also Richard's Chancellor.

King Richard left the Tower and was rowed down river to talk to the rebels, keeping his boat a safe distance from the banks. The rebels demanded the heads of Sudbury and Gaunt, clearly frightening the young King. Then the defenders of London were betrayed by John Horne and Alderman Sibley, who let down the drawbridge so that the rebels could cross the river and enter London.

Once inside the city, Wat Tyler could no longer control his mob, who went on an orgy of looting. John of Gaunt's Savoy Palace had its wine cellar plundered and was then burnt down; men from Rochester were said to have stolen Gaunt's strongbox containing £1,000. The inmates of the Fleet Prison were released.

Tyler had set up his headquarters at Mile End where he could meet with the men from Essex. King Richard, with no alternatives, agreed to meet him there. Tyler demanded the abolition of serfdom and of feudal services, to which the King seemed to assent.

Some of the rebels were satisfied by what they had achieved and went home. Unfortunately others were still seeking revenge. The guards at the Tower were surprised by some of them, who managed to force their way in. When they burst into the Countess of Kent's bedroom she fainted, but worse lay in store for Sudbury and Sir Robert Hales, the Treasurer. As soon as the rebels were in the Tower they went to the chapel, where Sudbury had started to say mass. Before he could finish both he and Hales were dragged out and executed. Their heads were put on poles and carried round London.

The sober aims of the original Kent protests were drowned in uncontrolled violence. Racism surfaced, and 160 Flemings were butchered – 35 of them being dragged out of St Martin in the Vintry church and beheaded.

The next day King Richard again met Tyler, this time at Smithfield. According to tradition, Tyler leant forward during the negotiations and put his hand on the bridle of the King's horse. Other accounts suggest that Tyler drank beer and spat on the ground, prompting one of the King's men – who came from Kent – to say that he knew Tyler to be a thief and a highwayman. Perhaps Tyler was warned off as he came too near the King, but something happened to make him angry. Tyler drew his dagger and stepped towards the King. Walworth, thinking Richard to be in danger, warned Tyler off sharply. Tyler then tried to stab the Lord Mayor, who had sensibly decided to put on chain mail beneath his outer garments. Walworth struck back, and then John Standwick (or Standish) dealt Tyler a mortal blow.

The killing of their leader could have caused the rebels to avenge themselves on Richard, Walworth and the other lords. Instead the young King rode forward and declared, 'I will be your chief and captain.' Richard's presence of mind allowed the Royal forces time to gather sufficient strength to deter any further violence, and the Kent rebels were led peacefully back through London and across the Thames. Walworth, meanwhile, traced Tyler's body to St Bartholomew's Hospital; he had it dragged out and beheaded. The head was taken to Richard, then put up on London Bridge in place of Sudbury's.

Jack Straw was soon captured and executed but it took another month for John Ball to be caught in Coventry. Chief Justice

Belknap went to Kent to try those known to have led the revolt, but overall punishments were mild for the period. Richard himself visited the county, travelling through Ospringe, Canterbury and Sandwich.

The Peasants' Revolt died out with a few last sparks. In September 1381 a revolt was planned in Maidstone against John of Gaunt, but came to nothing. The revolt was over, but it was only the first taste of a 200 year period in which the men of Kent developed a rebellious reputation.

CHARLES DICKENS

W HAT, one wonders, would Charles Dickens have made of his beloved Rochester today? Even in his last few months he loved to explore the old city which he portrayed as 'Cloisterham' in his final novel, *The Mystery of Edwin Drood.* He enjoyed poking around the murky edges of the river Medway and the dark corners of the cathedral, where he felt the touch of encroaching death.

Charles Dickens was not born in Kent but at Portsmouth, where his father John was a clerk in the Navy Pay Office. His talent for creating stories was probably inherited from his grandmother, who had been a maid at Crewe Hall and was the model for Mrs Rouncewell in *Bleak House.*

In 1817 John Dickens was transferred to Chatham and the family moved into Ordnance Terrace there. This was a nice home, then not facing the railway station, but in 1822 the family had to move to the less attractive Brook district of the town. Young Charles became familiar with the landscape of the Medway towns, often walking over the hill to Rochester or down to the river, on which convict hulks were then moored.

His youthful idyll in Kent was cut short in 1823 when the family moved to Camden. Money problems were looming and his mother's attempt to help by starting a private school foundered when no pupils attended. Such was the family's despera-

The church at Stoke. Lonely churches and muddy creeks give the Kent marshes their character, and were the inspiration and setting for much of Charles Dickens' writing.

tion that Charles was sent to work in a blacking warehouse at the age of twelve. It was to be perhaps the most formative experience of his life – 'No words can express the secret agony of my soul,' he later wrote about this time.

Even young Charles' meagre wages could not save his father from imprisonment in the Marshalsea for debt, an experience which he used later in *Little Dorrit*. The family was rescued, however, by the death of his grandmother, who left some money that enabled John Dickens to leave the prison. But fear of poverty and debt troubled Charles for the rest of his life. It could be said that he worked himself to death for fear of repeating his father's problems.

In 1827 Dickens became a solicitor's clerk and in 1832 a reporter, working on such journals as the *True Sun* and the

Morning Chronicle. During this time he fell hopelessly in love with Maria Beadnell, who tormented him endlessly. Some see in her the model for various unapproachable Dickensian women and the unhappy love lives of young men such as Pip in *Great Expectations.*

In 1833 Dickens discovered a talent for writing short sketches for magazines and in 1836 these were published as *Sketches by Boz* – his first book. This offered Dickens a degree of security and enabled him to marry Kate Hogarth in April 1836. Kate has often been depicted as dull and uninteresting, but she bore Dickens ten children over the years of their marriage so she can hardly have had the time or the opportunity to thrive as a social animal. For their honeymoon they stayed in a cottage at Chalk near Gravesend.

Dickens threw himself into writing anything he could that would earn money. He began editing *Bentley's Miscellany* and wrote *Pickwick* and *Oliver Twist* more or less at the same time. Many of his novels were written in instalments for magazines, often with Dickens having no idea how the story would end! During the same period he became very fond of Kate's sister Mary, and her sudden death left him very saddened.

In 1837 Dickens began to make regular visits to Broadstairs, where he was able to do much of his writing. Most of *Bleak House* was written while staying there, and much of *The Old Curiosity Shop.*

By 1838 Dickens was so busy he found difficulty in getting the time to open his letters. He was also becoming a social success, much in demand at the dinner tables of the wealthy. Leigh Hunt gives us an idea of why this was in his description of Dickens' impact on a room of people: 'What a face to meet in a drawing room. It has the life and soul in it of 50 human beings.'

In 1841 Dickens considered standing for Parliament, having had experience as a political reporter, but decided he had neither the time nor the money. He was being cheated by pirated editions of his books and in 1843 *Martin Chuzzlewit* proved a commercial disappointment. He had, though, found that public speaking was both enjoyable and lucrative.

A trip to America in 1842 was not a great success, including five days of seasickness as well. He came back exhausted, and went to Broadstairs to recuperate.

In the mid-1840s his finances began to improve. The idea of producing a Christmas story was very successful and *The Cricket* was dramatised at twelve London theatres concurrently. *Dombey & Son* was a success too and Dickens was confident enough to begin his own newspaper, the *Daily News*, in 1846. This allowed him to champion his own views, such as opposition to capital punishment.

David Copperfield, the book which allowed Dickens to exorcise his past, began to appear in 1849 and opened a new phase in his writing. In 1850 he started *Household Words*, a magazine born out of idleness during a Broadstairs holiday and intended to reach the family homes of the poorer classes.

In February 1857 Dickens got possession of Gads Hill Place, in the country halfway between Gravesend and Rochester. While it was fitted out he stayed with his wife at Waite's Hotel in Gravesend, some of his time there being occupied on *Little Dorrit*.

After the family moved into Gads Hill, one of their visitors was Hans Christian Andersen. He stayed several weeks and one day Mrs Dickens found him face down in the clover, weeping. She thought someone must have died, but it was merely that Andersen had just read a savage review of his work.

Dickens was very friendly with Wilkie Collins, the mystery novelist, by 1856. Collins had a reputation as a compulsive womaniser and Dickens' marriage was already unhappy, so Collins' influence may have been behind Dickens' affair with a young actress named Ellen Ternan. Only 16 when he met her, she was apparently crying because she was being made to wear a costume which she considered too revealing. Cynics have said the tears were for the benefit of Dickens, since she had worn the costume before.

Charles Dickens at the age of 56. His face was described by Leigh Hunt as having 'the life and soul in it of 50 human beings'.

Dickens bought Ellen Ternan a house in Peckham, but was unsure what to do about his wife. Eventually it was Kate Dickens' own sister, Georgina, who decreed that she should live in London apart from the family and with very restricted access to the children. Georgina ruled the roost at Gads Hill, where Dickens did most of his writing in a garden chalet, and the situation caused something of a scandal.

Dickens worked on *Great Expectations* in 1860–1, bringing

together many of the influences of his Kent childhood and his time at Gads Hill. The atmosphere of the Marshes is crucial to the book, and Dickens spent many hours wandering over to Lower Higham and Cliffe while living in the area. Miss Havisham's house was based on Satis House in Rochester.

In 1865 Dickens went to Paris with Ellen Ternan and on the journey home was involved in the terrible railway accident at Staplehurst, when the boat train was derailed due to work on the track. Dickens gave brandy to several of the injured and was horrified to see them die in his arms.

A tour of America in 1867–8 earned him about £20,000, but his old fear of financial disaster continued to drive him onwards. In 1868 he began another tour of Britain, reading selected extracts from his books and this time including the murder of Nancy from *Oliver Twist*. The schedule was too much for him, and Dickens had to return to Gads Hill to rest.

There he worked on *Edwin Drood*, invoking images of Rochester under the guise of 'Cloisterham'. 'A city of another and bygone time is Cloisterham,' he wrote, 'with its hoarse cathedral-bell, its hoarse rooks hovering about the cathedral tower . . .'

On 15th March 1870 he gave his last reading and shortly afterwards was awarded a baronetcy, becoming Sir Charles Dickens of Gads Hill. When he met Queen Victoria she kept him standing – in agony – for one and a half hours, though she did him the honour of standing too. She gave him a copy of her own book on the Scottish highlands and asked for a complete set of his works in return!

Dickens spent his last day in the chalet at Gads Hill, working on *Edwin Drood*. During dinner that night he suffered a stroke and never recovered. The great artist Millais sketched him while he was dying. Dickens died on 9th June 1870, aged only 58; Britain's greatest novelist had worn himself out.

INDEX